HOW
TO
GIVE
GOOD
PHONE

HOW TO GIVE GOOD PHONE

Telephone Techniques to
Increase Your Power,
Profits and Performance

by LISA COLLIER COOL

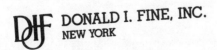 DONALD I. FINE, INC.
NEW YORK

Copyright © 1988 by Lisa Collier Cool

All rights reserved, including the right of reproduction in whole or in part in any form. Published in the United States of America by Donald I. Fine, Inc. and in Canada by General Publishing Company Limited.

Library of Congress Catalogue-in-Publication Data

Cool, Lisa Collier, 1952–
   How to give good phone.

   1. Telephone in business. 2. Telephone etiquette.
I. Title.
HF5541.T4C66   1988   651.7'3   87-81422
ISBN: 1-55611-050-2 (pbk. : alk. paper)

Manufactured in the United States of America

10 9 8 7 6 5 4 3 2

Design by Stanley S. Drate/Folio Graphics Co. Inc.

To my three favorite phone voices,
John, Alison and Georgia

CONTENTS

ACKNOWLEDGMENTS

For their valuable contributions to this book, I'd like to thank:

Oscar Collier, my father and agent, for sharing his artful negotiating tactics with me.

George Coleman and Don Fine, for making my phone fantasies into reality.

Pete Caminiti, Muriel Fox, Nick Mancino, Robert Saft, Elizabeth Tener, and Jerome Tuccille, for offering their time and telephone techniques.

The librarians at New Rochelle and Pelham libraries, for their interest and courteous assistance.

INTRODUCTION

Whether it's a black rotary dial phone or part of a high tech telecommunications network, the telephone is *the* essential business tool. At the touch of a finger, it can give you immediate access to any one of a billion other phone users—customers and clients, potential employers or sources of financing and important contacts anywhere on the globe.

As a literary agent and journalist, I've spent much of my business life on the telephone, interviewing prospective clients and news sources, offering advice and coping with crises, making pitches for my own and others' literary projects, negotiating contracts and cultivating new customers.

No matter which business you're in, telephone mastery is equally crucial to your success. The average person spends one entire year of his or her life talking on the telephone—a staggering 8,760 hours—but in many careers, like mine, phone calls consume an even greater number of working hours. Clearly telephone talk is far from cheap; it represents a substantial investment of our time *and* money—we can expect to shell out nearly fifty thousand dollars for those calls.

Despite the vast power that's quite literally waiting at our fingertips, few of us fully exploit the potential of the phone. What inspired me to write this book were the frequent confessions I heard from business associates about their telephone hang-ups: the calls that weren't returned, the problems of obstructive secretaries, the time wasted languishing in the limbo of "hold," the sales pitch that went sour, the failure of their calls to generate the desired action.

Such failures of communication are quite common since few of us really take charge of the telephone—or consciously use it to increase our power, profits and performance on the job. To make each call genuinely productive, we need potent techniques that guarantee that our messages are received and acted upon. But to make the telephone the instrument of your business success, you must do more than control the content of the call—you must also learn to reliably project a winning impression of yourself to the listener.

Since we put ourselves on the line every time we lift the receiver to make or accept a call, telephone success isn't just a matter of technique, but one of personal style. Developing telephone expertise is a voyage of self-discovery, as you learn to package your personality traits—both positive and negative— for maximum impact as part of an appealing phone image.

Part One of this book will help you achieve a more powerful phone personality. As you work toward mastery of the art of self-expression, you'll learn how to make an immediate positive impression, overcome common psychological barriers to effective communication, direct your telephone "traffic flow" for more profitable phone time, defend yourself against power players on the other end of the line and heat up even the coldest calls with the fire of total self-confidence.

Part Two will reveal the secret of how to spend more of your time "dialing for dollars," as you deliver persuasive sales pitches, create the right impression on powerful new contacts, gain shrewder buys and larger sales, turn the phone into a negotiating weapon and close deals quickly and satisfactorily.

An equally important—but often overlooked—key to phone success is the skill of creative listening. I'll show how to recognize and decipher hidden conversational clues to the other person's secret desires and exploit them to increase sales, establish rapid rapport with strangers, triumph in negotiation, unmask deceitful job applicants and business associates and hear *exactly* what the other person is really saying.

Also included are practical strategies for common calling situations: the fine art of creative complaining, getting fast action from the tardy, coping with crisis calls and other tricky calls and finding the right line to take in any business call.

In Part Three you'll discover how to extract further profits and greater performance from your phone. Here you'll explore the rapidly growing world of electronic rendezvous, and learn just how to get your computer online for high tech networking and high speed information access; as well as how to enjoy cheaper—and more efficient—talk by selecting the best phone paraphernalia and services for your business needs.

With the right strategies, equipment and mental outlook, you *can* talk your way to the top—and this book will show you exactly how. Not only will your message register and impress, but you'll leave your audience sold on you—the consummate communicator.

PART ONE:
POWER

Developing a
Winning
Telephone
Personality

MAKING
CONTACT

The time: Monday morning, 8:45 A.M. The place: your office. As you walk in, you hear your phone ringing. Racing over to your desk, you snatch up the receiver and identify yourself.

"Greetings," booms an unfamiliar baritone. "Had your coffee yet?"

"Who's this?" you say, struggling to remove your overcoat without dropping the phone.

"Old Tom says you might be able to make a lot of money for me," the caller says, raising his already loud voice a few decibel levels. "But first, could you fill me in on your background?"

You obligingly launch into your resume, wondering exactly why you are trying to sell yourself to this unidentified caller. You are also racking your brains trying to figure out just who "Old Tom" is. Right now the only Tom who comes to mind is a neighbor whose cat routinely leaves muddy footprints on your car.

"Well, I suppose you'll do," the caller says with a hint of a snicker. "The reason I thought of your organization is that,

3

well, a few months ago I had a slipped disc—have you ever had one?"

"No, but I'd appreciate it if you'd tell me who this is," you say a bit sharply.

"No mystery about that," the caller chortles. "It's Neil Bodkin. That's Neil with an e-i, not the other way around. People often get it wrong. And Bodkin is B-o-d-k-i-n."

"What's the purpose of your call, Mr. Bodkin?" Glancing at your watch, you see that you have five minutes until your first appointment.

"Ah yes, my little proposition. Well, back when I had that slipped disc—the second time it's happened . . ." He drones on for another three minutes, leaving you more bewildered than ever.

"Sorry, I've got to run," you snap as your secretary buzzes to announce your visitor. "I've got someone waiting to see me."

"Oh, this will only take a minute," Bodkin cajoles.

"Some other time, perhaps. Bye." You replace the receiver firmly.

A few days later, to your dismay, you find a letter from Bodkin in the morning mail. You consider discarding it unread, but seeing that it is mercifully brief, you begin scanning the contents.

"Old Tom" is revealed in the first paragraph to be T. J. Harris, an important buyer you've been wooing unsuccessfully for three months. Your interest increases as you read a succinct description of a promising product Bodkin has developed, and by the time you get to the third paragraph, which offers your firm exclusive marketing rights at an attractive discount, you're sold.

As a literary agent, I've often witnessed similar Jekyll-to-Hyde transformations. I've known authors who were masterful at pitching their work on paper yet couldn't deliver a message with equal impact when the medium was the telephone; businessmen and women who had put together a powerful visual image through adroit dress and office decor yet faltered on the phone without these props to bolster them.

The problem wasn't faulty communication skills—after all, these were publishing *professionals*—but a basic misconception about the nature of the phone. Although most of us realize the importance of the right look in business—we dress for success, plant subtle status cues in our offices and hire designers to create distinctive stationery and corporate logos—when we lift the receiver we forget about image and imagine that we're "just talking."

YOUR PHONE PERSONALITY

We've all had the disconcerting experience of finally meeting one of our telephone acquaintances face-to-face and discovering that his or her appearance isn't as we'd imagined. This common occurrence illustrates the power of a voice to conjure up a vivid characterization of the speaker in the mind of the listener. One voice might register as "mature and distinguished"; another as "small but aggressive." While each of us might interpret these images into different mental pictures, our responses are still dictated by qualities projected by the caller.

Over the phone, some facets of your personality are hidden, others highlighted. However, even though you may come across rather differently on the phone than you do in person, with the right approach you can score as positive an impression vocally as you do visually. Or your effectiveness might be improved—I have several business associates who give fantastic phone, but create an undistinguished or even negative impression in person.

When someone meets you face-to-face for the first time,

he's reacting to a complete package: your style of dress, degree of physical attractiveness, characteristic expressions and gestures and the environment in which he encounters you. Since vision is our dominant sense, a pleasing appearance can distract attention away from any minor deficiencies in your voice or delivery.

On the phone, however, your impact depends totally on what you say, and most importantly, *how* you say it. Communication is more intimate when the first contact occurs by phone, without visual cues to guide him, all the other party "sees" is the self-image you project. While ineffective callers unconsciously allow their inner fears and insecurities to be revealed, the key to telephone mastery is to *control* your underlying message.

While it's possible to conceal whatever secret doubts you may harbor about yourself, the easier and more practical tactic is to eliminate them. Tell yourself that you're "just a salesperson" or that most of your prospects will turn you down, and it will be all but impossible to convey enthusiasm and confidence when you pitch your goods or service. Instead, take the attitude of Joe Girard, listed in the *Guiness Book of World Records* as the world's top car salesman: "I don't have any big secrets. I simply sell the world's best product. *I sell Joe Girard.*"

THE ELEMENTS OF STYLE

What kind of product are you? To start building a distinctive image for yourself, advertising executive Jane Trahey, author of *Jane Trahey on Women and Power,* writes: "Decide if you're Dom Perignon or whether you're a raw and splendid chianti." Whether you opt to be the exclusively elegant "21" Club or to project the comfortable reliability of a Holiday Inn, your image should present you in a flattering but basically truthful light.

Since the most memorable images are basically one-liners, you have to sift through your complex and sometimes contradictory mix of characteristics to select your most saleable quality. Almost any trait—except an indecisive or hesitant tone—can form the basis of an effective telephone image. A sober, thoughtful style can imbue those you call with confidence in your judgment, while an impassioned enthusiasm can fire up cold calls.

Your name or choice of job description can contribute to your image. Literary agent Irving Lazar undoubtedly owes some of his success to his nickname of "Swifty," with its connotation of rapid results. Or consider the career counselor who introduces herself as a "career-builder" and the insurance salesman who tells his prospects that he's a "premium-maximizer." The former has chosen a tag phrase that encapsulates the anticipated results of using her services, while the latter has added an element of mystery to his image.

An image can also be constructed around a calling situation. When Mary joined the collection department of a large bank, she first tried the standard tactics of intimidation, but found that her group of delinquent debtors considered her threats more of a challenge than a call for action. Realizing that she just didn't come across as a tough guy, she adopted the opposite tack. She started each call by greeting the debtor with exquisite courtesy, then requested the tardy payment in a mild, pleasant voice. Her quiet persistence paid off: The debtors found themselves wanting to please this agreeable caller by sending off their payment more promptly.

What if your dominant trait is a negative one? How do you overcome the impression left by an aggressive manner, a flamboyant style, a hasty temper? Often an apparently undesirable trait can be repackaged into a winning image. Consider Charles, who manages a small import firm. He's loud, critical, demanding and prone to nag. Realizing that he'll never make a cent through charm, he's mastered a technique of presenting his points with emphatic brevity, blasting past objections and closing the deal.

FIFTEEN SECONDS TO IMPACT

How long does it take to establish an image? Studies show that within the first fifteen seconds of acquaintance, we form a surprisingly strong and durable impression of someone new, whether the first contact takes place by phone or through an in-person meeting. And once an impression is formed, we're resistant to changing our ideas about that person. Our tendency is to look for information that confirms our original perception and to disregard contradictory signals.

Assuming that we speak at the average rate of 140 words per minute that means that the first thirty-five words we utter during an introductory call are the key to a winning phone image. One sales trainer refers to this period as the time when a caller must "lift the curse," since many businesspeople consider a call from a stranger, especially if he's got something to sell, an unwelcome intrusion into their workday. However, amid their suspicion or hostility there's also some curiosity: Could it be that there's something to be gained from speaking to you?

That the effective phone personality knows how to exploit this natural human response was illustrated to me today by my reactions to two sales calls I received from strangers. The first caller's opening line was: "Lisa, our salesman will be in your area next week to show our new line of replacement windows, and we'd like to put you down for Friday." The other caller started off by saying: "Mrs. Cool, this is Bill Tanner of Merrill Lynch. Do you have a minute to talk? [I replied in the affirmative.] I'd like to explain an investment program that would reduce your taxes substantially."

Within the ten to fifteen seconds she took to deliver these introductory remarks, the first caller dramatically reduced the odds of doing business with me by her off-putting presentation. The use of my first name and her failure to identify herself or her firm at the onset of the call struck me as rude, while her sales message—that I should buy now because it was convenient for the salesman to call—failed to arouse my interest. Her lack of consideration triggered an immediate refusal on my part.

The second caller also used less than thirty words but scored an excellent impression. Here's a breakdown of his introductory technique:

• **Identifying the recipient.** Starting off by greeting the listener by name both establishes that you've reached the correct party and ensures attention. By using the more formal mode of address, "Mrs. Cool," the second caller also conveys an image of courtesy by using the appropriate etiquette of an introductory call.

• **Identifying yourself.** By referring to himself as "Bill Tanner" rather than "William Tanner" or "Mr. Tanner," the caller establishes an impression of friendliness. He's inviting intimacy without being brash about it. He also avoids the mistake of putting too much emphasis on his own name at this early point, recognizing that he hasn't yet provided the motivation for me to desire to learn it permanently.

• **Identifying the firm.** Since this company already enjoys a national reputation, stating its name is sufficient. For less well known organizations, a brief description is helpful: "a telecommunications network." Other identification, such as the name of a third party who suggested the call, can also be provided at this point.

• **Establishing convenience.** By showing respect for my time— "Do you have a minute to talk?"—he politely asks my permission to continue, reinforcing the impression he's already created of politeness and consideration. He's ensured that he'll be able to speak his piece without a constant struggle to hold the attention of a prospect who's anxious to end the call.

• **Getting down to business.** Now that the preliminaries are out of the way, he's distilled his message into an enticing hook that arouses curiosity as to the rest of the presentation.

PEAK PHONE PERFORMANCES

This kind of positive impact is not accidental. During her first six months in business, an employment agent I know noticed a puzzling pattern: She placed nearly twice as many workers in the afternoon as the morning, despite dividing her telephone time equally between the two periods. By taping a day's worth of calls, she uncovered the explanation: She was rehearsing on the morning prospects, while her afternoon calls represented the polished and perfected performance.

Most of us are not "on" all of the time, yet we can't afford to write off certain calling hours merely because they don't correspond to our natural peaks of ability. Instead, we need a technique of summoning up the proper mood and message on cue so that we're always ready to attack the phone with confidence and score the desired result.

The first move is to crystallize your objective. Bob, the owner of a software marketing firm, has been frustrated in his efforts to secure a prompt mortgage commitment from the banker he's approached about financing a business property. Although he's called several times to urge speed, the conversation ends with vague reassurances from the banker that "the file is being completed" and that he'll have his answer "soon."

What he eventually realized was that he was asking the wrong questions. Once he pinpointed his goal as that of determining exactly which documents the banker lacked, he was then able to contact the two credit references himself and convince them to send the required information out that very day. Forty-eight hours later he had his loan.

A soft drink distributor who found herself deluged with excuses every time she called a certain overdue account found her difficulties in keeping the conversation on track ended when she taped a note to her phone reading: "Yes, but when are you going to send the money?" She found this ploy so effective that she made a regular practice of creating such one-sentence reminders before placing any important call.

Once you've captured the reason for the call into a succinct message, you'll want to deliver it in an appealing manner. One tactic that many telephone users never think of employing is a "telephone smile." Not only does a pleasant expression help build rapport in person, but it transmits an equally positive impression across phone lines. Your listener really does hear the smile in your voice.

There may be a scientific basis for this effect. Researchers at the University of California in San Francisco have discovered that imitating the facial expression associated with a particular emotion actually produces the same physical changes in the body as the genuine emotion: Fake a frown and in ten seconds your heart rate and skin temperature will rise. And if a look can launch such strong physical reactions, just imagine how it affects your attitude.

GOOD VIBRATIONS

Once you've mastered the technique of evoking a positive first impression quickly, build on this promising beginning by designing your main presentation to stimulate strong rapport and interest on the part of the listener.

Here's how:

• **Position your ideas for impact.** Studies indicate that 85 percent of what you say will be forgotten within an hour after the conclusion of the conversation. To ensure that your most important points—not the incidental details—are what's recalled later, present your most interesting idea *first* and reserve your second best point as a closing clincher. Choreograph the remaining ideas into a series of mini-climaxes—the revelation of each new idea—followed by a lower-keyed elaboration of its details.

• **Personalize the presentation.** Use your listener's name and that of her firm at strategic moments in the conversation to gain increased interest. Keep the conversation focused on how your ideas apply to her specific situation—not on your own opinions and experiences. Enhance the effect by occasionally using some insider slang or jargon unique to her industry to show her that you speak her language.

• **Pay attention and profit.** The recipient of your call will not only judge you by your speaking style, but also by how well you listen to him. Most of us aren't as attentive as we might be, since we can think four times faster than the other person can speak, it's easy to get lost in our own mental chatter. This is especially true during an initial call, since our thoughts may be preoccupied with what we plan to say *next*, not what the other is saying *now*.

Not only does inattention tarnish your image and annoy the other person, but it can cost you the opportunity to locate the other person's hidden hot buttons. Buried in his stated objection there may be a valuable clue as to his true fears or desires. By hearing both his words—and the meaning behind them—you could then shift the thrust of your ideas to align them more closely with those of the listener.

• **Get the listener into the act.** By encouraging the listener to take an active role in the dialog, you'll gain both valuable feedback and increased interest on his part. Gauge his reactions by tossing him a question from time to time. Use a combination of yes-or-no queries and more open-ended questions that compel him to spin his replies out at greater length.

• **Accentuate the positive.** The essence of building rapport is establishing areas of agreement and downplaying conflicts. If your ideas are met with resistance, avoid the temptation to turn the conversation into a debate. Instead, defuse the criticism by first agreeing with it, then offering a solution. A consistently upbeat tone will also reduce the potential for evoking negative emotions or responses in the listener.

• **Make friendly overtures.** Since we tend to like people who seem to like us, giving the listener a verbal stroke occasionally will make him feel that *he's* performing well. When he asks a question, for example, you might, if appropriate, praise him for having the perception to raise this particular point; or you might instead voice your sincere and enthusiastic agreement with one of his remarks.

• **Give the listener his money's worth.** It's your dime (or quarter) that's financing the call, but remember that the other person is contributing something even more valuable—his time. Give him what he wants—a profitable conversation— through concise organization; then add a touch of razzle-dazzle—your entertaining phone personality—as a rewarding bonus.

Consider an introductory call a form of courtship. Without being obsequious, subtly convey the message that you are trying to impress him and that you consider him a valued potential contact. If you can then convince him that you're bringing an attractive dowry of useful ideas, you've provided the basis of a mutually worthwhile business relationship.

LEAVE THEM HUNGRY FOR MORE

What's the best way to close a sale? According to one top salesman, the secret is to close early and to close often. The same principle applies to any introductory call whose purpose is to generate action. Your first two or three points may be enough to produce the desired result; if so, further elaboration is overkill.

Let the other person know early in the conversation exactly what move you're expecting from her, and repeat the information from time to time. As soon as she indicates willingness to act, *stop talking*. Sticking doggedly to your script could result in your buying back what you'd already sold by allowing the other person further time to reflect on the wisdom of her decision.

Even if you're not pushing for action in this call, there's still a good reason to probe periodically to determine if the call's purpose has been achieved. By closing the call before the other person's interest has evaporated you'll depart on a high note and not be remembered as a visitor who overstayed his welcome.

There are several good ways to wrap up your call smoothly. If a decision was reached or an appointment made, repeat the salient facts to avoid misunderstanding: "I'll phone you Thursday morning at ten o'clock." Another method is to close with friendly remarks like, "It was great talking to you" or "I'll be in touch soon." An easy and courteous close that works well on most calls is to thank the other person for his time, information or decision to act. This sounds warm and clearly conclusive and leaves a residue of good feelings after you hang up.

2

ONE-MINUTE TELEPHONE MANAGEMENT

Are you consistently using your telephone profitably? Odds are that you're not: A study by Accountemps revealed that on average we waste one out of every three hours we spend at work. Since the typical phone user can expect to spend 8,760 hours on the phone in his lifetime—and many business users will far exceed this figure—that ratio translates to 365 workdays devoted to pointless phone calling. The annual expense to American industry from its employees' mismanagement of the phone is conservatively estimated at $50 million.

PRIME PHONE TIME

By eliminating all inefficiency you could theoretically boost your phone productivity by 50 percent and gain the equivalent of a year and a half of additional working time to devote to money-making activities. However, recognizing that even the most consummate communicator will unavoidably find himself ensnared in playing telephone tag with elusive associates or languishing on hold, a more realistic objective would be to cut dead time in half.

Your greatest opportunity to realize substantial savings of time and money, however, lies in the other two-thirds of your calls—the ones that are already productive. Here's why. An economic axiom called the Pareto principle (named after Vilfredo Pareto, a nineteenth-century economist) holds that 80 percent of the value of a group of items is generally concentrated in just 20 percent of those items. Applying this rule to phone calls suggests that 80 percent of our results are achieved by 20 percent of our words, implying that we could accomplish almost as much in one-fifth the time.

Here's how to streamline your phone use.

TARGET YOUR TIME

End each business day by preparing a list of the calls you need to make the next day, jotting down a specific goal for each one: "Get price quote" or "Discuss the HBJ situation." Some calls may prove difficult to define in a single phrase because their purpose is subtle and complex. You might be phoning to stroke a client you suspect of being on the verge of defecting, plant a few seeds that you hope will grow into a future deal or solidify your relationship with a new business associate. Such calls can be characterized with all-purpose labels like "build goodwill" or "promote future growth."

Arrange the list of projected calls by priority—your priorities, not someone else's. Don't decide to call Mr. Z first because he's the worst nuisance; call Ms. X who was just hired as vice-president at one of your biggest accounts. However, avoid the common pitfall of putting off unpleasant but urgent calls. Plan instead to deliver the bad tidings or brave the confrontation *first*. As one of my clients used to say: "Eat a live toad every morning, and nothing worse will happen to you all day."

Schedule the most important calls for the prime morning calling hours of your industry (generally 9:00 A.M. to 10:00 A.M.) before everyone escapes to meetings or long lunches, gets tied up on the other line or becomes distracted by other business. If the person you're calling isn't in, you've still accomplished something positive by putting your name on the top of his or her call-back list. It's a common rule that the first call received is the first returned.

If your schedule includes many long distance calls, plan on calling east in the morning, west in the afternoon. One West Coast film producer I know likes to brag how he can cram three days work into one: "At 8:00 A.M. I can just catch the end of the European business day, at lunchtime I start hitting them in New York and by the end of the day I've caught up with the locals."

Complete your preparations by assembling the relevant files or notes you'll need for each call. Many potentially profitable calls wind up as inconclusive discussions simply because one person lacks a vital piece of information the other needs if she's to take action or reach a decision. At best, results are held up until the missing link can be supplied during an additional call; at worst, an opportunity can slip away during this delay as second thoughts creep in, or more enticing blandishments are offered by someone else.

YOUR TELEPHONE LOG

A written log of your telephone calls is a valuable tool for evaluating—and increasing—your efficiency. Not only will this record provide a snapshot of exactly how your telephone time is spent, but it's a handy reminder of what you've already achieved and what sort of follow-up is needed during future calls. And if a misunderstanding ensues, your log will help settle disputes and quite possibly prevent costly lawsuits.

Here's what to log (see illustration 2-1 for sample log page):

• **Incoming or outgoing?** You'll want a complete record of all calls made and received each day, whether these calls are handled by you or taken for you by an assistant.

• **Time spent on the call.** This will help you detect any holes in your telephone techniques—and make appropriate adjustments in the future. In the sample log provided in illustration 2-1, for example, the entries show that its writer can handle a negotiating call with dispatch (eight minutes), but is ineffective at getting action (after twenty-three minutes of discussion he still failed to resolve the problem) and at terminating trivial calls (he devoted ten minutes to hearing a sales pitch that didn't interest him).

• **Person Called/Caller.** Enter the full name, title and company affiliation of new callers; a week from now you may have forgotten just who "K. Hall" was. Familiar callers should be identified by full name to prevent possible confusion between the various Toms or Janes of your acquaintance.

• **Time of call.** After you've kept the log for several days, you'll gain a feeling for the ebb and flow of your telephone traffic, which will help you schedule your other work to avoid conflicts with your peak calling hours.

• **Goal of call.** For outgoing calls, enter your objective before placing the call, then concentrate on realizing it in the fewest possible words. For incoming calls, indicate the apparent purpose of the call.

• **Result.** How effective were you at reaching the correct party and at achieving the purpose of your call? For incoming calls, did the caller accomplish his stated purpose? Were you sold on his ideas or willing to act on his message? Studying both your own tactics and those of others is a good way to expand your repertoire of techniques while also identifying and eliminating phone habits that may be making a poor impression.

• **Comments.** How could you have handled this call more effectively? If the call was incoming, how would you score the caller: Did she get to the point quickly, capture and hold your interest and communicate well? Or did you rate the call a waste of time? Why?

SCRUTINIZE YOUR INBOUND TRAFFIC

What you'll quickly realize is that incoming calls are often the greatest time-wasters. You may also observe the 80/20 rule in action: Typically 80 percent of your calls will come from people who produce only 20 percent of your profits. When you place the call, your energy is directed at obtaining some goal that's of value to you, but an incoming call may seduce you away from gainful efforts to hear a message that's of little or no interest. To minimize the time spent on these distracting interruptions, aim at terminating all but the most complex and important conversations in three minutes or less.

Here's a timetable for compressing communication:

First minute: Determine the purpose of the call. Some callers will preface even the simplest idea with a long build-up. Cut through the verbiage and prompt your caller to get right to the point. A direct question often works well: "How can I help you?" or "What would you like me to do about this?"

Second minute: Once you understand the nature of the call, decide whether or not to proceed with it. If you are interested in what the caller has to say, let your voice convey enthusiasm. This will serve as a verbal nudge, letting the caller know that she now has your attention and should get down to business.

If the call doesn't interest you, be blunt. The longer you delay in saying, "No," the harder it will get. Each second builds up the hope of a favorable response and makes the caller more likely to argue with your decision. Cut into the conversation with a resolutely final statement: "I'm sorry, Mr. Johnson, but our board of directors has already considered the plan you propose and vetoed it. But thanks for touching base with me on these ideas."

Third minute: As soon as the conversation ceases to be fruitful, terminate it. For most of us, ending a conversation is far more difficult than initiating it. In a face-to-face talk it's easy to signal that the meeting has ended: You gather your belongings, stretch and rise from your chair, glance at your watch, signal for the check. On the telephone, where we must rely on verbal cues rather than body language, many of us find ourselves groping for the best means to extricate ourselves from a dialog that's already achieved its purpose.

Most inexperienced callers will slow down at the end of a conversation when they should speed up. Like a runner going into his final sprint at the end of a race, your picking up the pace of the conversation signals that the caller's time is up; it says, "I'm a busy person and must now turn my attention elsewhere." This ploy won't offend the caller; a brisk pace ends the call on an upbeat note, suggesting that you're a person of action rather than endless words. In addition, regular callers will come to recognize this as their cue to wrap up their ideas.

CALL SCREENING

Should you have someone else screen your calls? One survey of corporate presidents showed that a surprising 40 percent accepted their incoming calls themselves. One executive commented that as 95 percent of his calls proved important, it wasn't worth the effort to have an assistant filter out the trivial 5 percent. However, those at the top are rarely bothered by the requests for routine information and misdirected questions that can account for as much as 25 percent of the calling traffic of middle- or lower-level employees. In effect, a CEO's callers screen themselves before dialing.

By avoiding having their calls screened, these executives also avoided the potential dilemma of screening: how to filter out the unwelcome callers without alienating the desirable ones. Most of us find it offensive to be interrogated by an assistant as to the exact nature of our business before being connected; and those who have a touch of phone paranoia may consider such queries a form of rejection that makes them reluctant to brave the gauntlet a second time. Too impenetrable a net may put off important callers while seeming to be a challenge to aggressive unsolicited salespeople.

Since screening does increase your phone efficiency, the right approach is to offer it as a time-saving service established for the benefit of the *caller*. It's unavoidable that we'll sometimes be out or engaged in other important business when a call comes in, thus the offer of a knowledgeable assistant or secretary as a temporary stand-in expands your phone coverage. Callers now have the option, but not the obligation, of obtaining immediate results by dealing with your assistant. Or by leaving a detailed message they are assured that you'll brief yourself on the matter before your call-back—creating a more efficient conversation for both parties.

While this softened technique of screening will let some minor calls slip through, you can quickly terminate these calls yourself with the tactics described in the preceding section. Through a consistently courteous and helpful tone, your screener will gain the trust of frequent callers. Soon many of them will routinely request his or her assistance on trivial matters, reserving more important business to discuss personally with you. The presence of your screener will become a reminder that prompt assistance is always available at your office.

SCRIPTED FOR SUCCESS

Many businesspeople operate on the mistaken assumption that the nuances of telephone etiquette and procedure are intuitively obvious to their telephone delegate. Trusting your telephone image to an untrained delegate can be a dangerous mistake: As Machiavelli has observed, the prince is judged by his ambassador. In less than thirty seconds my positive impression of a certain dignified executive was forever shattered by the unfortunate candor of his call screener. She not only chose to reveal that the boss was in the bathroom but added quite gratuitously that he'd "been in there quite a while."

Giving your gatekeeper a script to follow will eliminate such embarrassing moments. While you may wish to add your own personal touches, here's a systematic approach to call screening.

Step One: Get ready. The call screener should be prepared for action with a generous supply of pens and note paper, plus copies of any frequently consulted reference materials, such as the list of direct dial numbers of others in the firm.

Step Two: Action. Your caller expects prompt attention. If possible, the screener should answer calls on the first ring—at latest by the third ring.

Step Three: Identification. Start each call by announcing the name of the firm, department or office, followed by the greeter's full name: "Bacon and Jones—Nancy Smith"; "Accounting Department—Brian Grossman"; "Ms. Conklin's office—Susan Kiefer."

If it's necessary to place a caller on hold immediately after answering, this should be done only after your screener has identified himself. It's annoying enough to hold without having to wonder if one's even reached the correct number. Stress the brevity of the wait: "Please hold for thirty seconds." After returning to the line, apologize for the delay.

Step Four: Offer assistance. Your assistant can now start the screening process by presenting an immediate opportunity for the caller to get down to business: "May I help you?" Callers merely wanting basic information are likely to capitalize on this offer, reducing the number of callers who actually request to speak with you.

Should the screener need to interrupt the call to get the necessary information, she should interrupt the call courteously: "Could you excuse me for a minute while I get the file, or would you like me to call you back when I have the figures in front of me?"

Step Five: Status report. If the call is received when you are either out or have requested that *all* calls be held, the fact of your unavailability should be announced before the screener asks for any further information. Callers may resent going through the whole rigmarole of explaining their business only to learn that you're not in after all. More suspicious callers may infer that you're actually in, but dodging their call.

For short absences, your screener should offer a diplomatic explanation of your absence and repeat her offer of assistance, including a reference to the possibility of leaving a message (the next section of this chapter will cover the specifics of taking a caller's message):

"I'm expecting him within the hour. May I help you, or give him a message?"

"She'll be in a meeting until three o'clock. Is there anything I can help you with now, or would you like to leave a message?"

For absences of more than a day, the screener should indicate the date of your return and offer both her own assistance and that of another member of the firm of comparable rank to yours:

"She'll be at the sales conference until May twenty-first. Is there something I could help you with, or would you like to be connected to Helga Smith, our sales and marketing manager?"

Step Six: Screening. If you're in, but wish to limit the number of interruptions to your work, you may opt to have the screener skip the status report for now and continue screening. The best ploy is to present the request as a diplomatic question: "Will she know what this call is in reference to?" While your screener may occasionally have the problem of brash salespeople claiming that you have a burning desire for their telephonic presence, nearly all callers will either reveal their name or provide an indication of why they are calling.

At this point, your screener may ferret out a misdirected call. She should then explain she believes that the call should be transferred and to whom she intends to connect the caller. A brief pause should follow for the caller's input; it's possible that he's already spoken with the other department or individual or has another sound reason for choosing to call your office.

Step Seven: Request the caller's name. If the caller states that his business is known to you but fails to identify himself, the screener must tactfully obtain his name. A direct request can strike some callers as rude or abrupt, so it's best to ask: "May I tell her who's calling?"

Your screener can then announce the call to you, and depending on your instructions, either return to the line saying that you'll be right on, or relay a message: "She says that she's eager to talk to you, but she's just finishing a meeting. What time can she return your call this afternoon?"

Step Eight: Complete the connection. Once your screener has established who's calling and why, she's ready to make a decision as to the disposition of the call. If the business clearly falls into her bailiwick, she can politely intercept the call by saying something like: "Mr. Fillmore told me that you would be calling to make an appointment, and I have his calendar right in front of me. What date did you have in mind?"

If these screening procedures fail to elicit the nature of the call, or the caller maintains that his business is confidential, the screener should be instructed to refer the call to you or offer to have you return it. It's far better to underscreen and let a few trivial calls get through than to overscreen and irk an important caller.

To avoid having important, expected calls ensnared in your screener's net, spend a few minutes each morning briefing her on crucial calls expected that day, and give her the names of any important new customers or contacts that you'd like to speak with right away. If you're anticipating routine calls from specific people, you may also wish to supply messages or written information that the screener can read to them when they call.

Step Nine: Present a winning image: Throughout the call, no matter what tone the caller takes, the screener should maintain an air of unruffled pleasantness. Use role-playing to rehearse your screener in such niceties as saying, "May I tell him who is calling?" rather than, "Who's calling?" Encourage liberal use of the caller's name and courtesies such as "please" and "thank you."

GETTING THE MESSAGE

What sort of image does your office present to those who call when you're out? Even a hint of disorganization or indifference from your delegates as they take a caller's message can transmit negative signals which the caller will associate with you. The skillful handling of messages, on the other hand, speaks well of your professionalism and general competence, even in your absence. Callers can leave the line confidently expecting that their words will be delivered to you accurately and promptly on your return.

Here are some tactics to ensure that the right message is received on *both* ends of the line:

• **Request messages tactfully.** Callers should be told that you are out before the screener requests the message. Some callers will prefer to place the call again, especially if they aren't already known to you. Others may not trust the screener to relay their message accurately or may consider their business too complex to reduce to a succinct message.

The best wording to coax a message from the reluctant caller is: "Will she know what this call is in reference to?" or "May I give her a message from you when she gets back?"

• **Offer the name and number option next.** As some callers will prefer not to be pinned down, this query should be made obliquely: "May I tell him who called?" or "Can I have her return your call later?" Even if the name is familiar to the screener, she should ask for a phone number: the caller may

Illustration 2.1 SAMPLE PHONE LOG

In/Out	Time Spent	Person Called/Caller	Time	Goal of Call	Result	Comments
Out	1 minute	L. Sheehan	9:00	Determine why contracts haven't arrived.	Not in—call back at 4:00	
Out	8 minutes	K. Hall	9:05	Complete negotiations on McBain project.	Explained reason for price decision, agreed upon terms.	
Out	23 minutes	S. James	9:20	Find out reason for delay of delivery.	Bogged down by excuses. Will call again tomorrow.	Call could have been greatly shortened by a more forceful tone on my part.
In	2 minutes	R. Hirschon	9:45	Wanted to get address of our advertising agency.		Was friendly, but got to the point right away.
In	10 minutes	Stockbroker can't remember his name	10:10	Trying to interest me in utilities.	Didn't interest me.	Sounded like he was reading his pitch.
In	10 minutes	K. Heller	10:25	Called to finalize negotiations on new contract.	Will call back after lunch.	Presented his ideas well, but spoke in a loud and unpleasant voice.

not be at his usual number or you may not have it readily at hand.

• **Verify the information provided:** To avoid garbled messages, the screener should recite back phone numbers and names for the caller's confirmation. The phonetic alphabet given below is helpful in distinguishing between similar-sounding letters, and gives a crisp military ring to the conversation:

ALPHA, BRAVO, CHARLIE, DELTA, ECHO, FOXTROT, GOLF, HO-TEL, INDIA, JULIET, KILO, LIMA, MIKE, NOVEMBER, OSCAR, PAPA, QUEBEC, ROMEO, SIERRA, TANGO, UNIFORM, VICTOR, WHISKEY, X-RAY, YANKEE, ZULU.

• **Keep a message checklist handy.** If preprinted message pads aren't used, each message should include: the caller's full name and business affiliation; phone number including the area code and extension (if any); message and action requested; time and date of the call; and the name or initials of the message-taker.

QUALITY CHECKS

Once you've trained your delegate in your preferred screening and message-handling routines, test them in operation by arranging to have a friend telephone your office during your absence while you listen in on an extension. If any flaws are detected, guide your screener through the correct procedures once you return to your office.

As she becomes adept at directing your telephone traffic and establishes herself as a familiar, reassuring presence to your regular callers, you'll find the two of you scoring consistently winning impressions through your telephone teamwork.

3

THE ART OF LISTENING

The master communicator recognizes that listening can often be more profitable than talking. J. P. Morgan was once interested in buying a Minnesota ore tract from the world's first billionaire, oilman John D. Rockefeller. Rockefeller dispatched his son, John D., Jr., to meet with the tycoon. "Well," demanded Morgan, "what is your price?" "Mr. Morgan," replied young Rockefeller, "I did not come here to sell. I understood that you wished to buy."

The object of this battle of wits was to secure the role of *listener* in the negotiations. Morgan's opening salvo implies, "I'm here to listen to your price"; while Rockefeller's counter is, "No, I'm here to listen to your offer." Both recognize the strategic value of silence: that having the *last* word—not the opening lines—will be the winning position in this contest.

A SENSE OF OPPORTUNITY

Most of us underrate the importance of listening. We approach conversation as a performance where points are scored with nimble verbal moves. Our language emphasizes the value of talk. We say admiringly that an associate "talks a good game"; that he's got "the gift of gab" or "a silver tongue" or can "talk anyone into anything." The idea of being a spellbinding speaker is definitely seductive; it appeals to our lust for action and victory.

Cultivating strong listening skills, however, will make you a more powerful communicator. Your close concentration on another's words is more than a courtesy that gains the speaker's gratitude; paying attention is a potential opportunity to reap even more rewarding payoffs of your own. When you're attuned to the subleties of seemingly innocuous statements, you'll hear hidden meanings and motivations of the speaker—and be able to use these signals to your advantage in selling, negotiating or persuading.

Careful listening also increases your telephone efficiency. Since the average speaking rate is 150 to 160 words per minute, while we can think 600 words per minute, only 25 percent of our mental capacity is required to record what's said. By dedicating the rest to exploring and reacting to those words—instead losing ourselves in distracting thoughts of our own—we enrich our listening, through extracting more meaning per minute, and our speaking, by targeting our words for greater impact.

A fear that can inhibit our ability to listen profitably is that of losing control of the conversation. Some novice salespeople, for example, are so determined not to be sidetracked by the prospect's ideas that they return to the prepared pitch the second he stops speaking, disregarding the intervening remarks. What they fail to realize is that silence can actually be a potent sales technique. As one master salesman put it: "While they talk, I listen and make the sale."

DIRECTING DISCUSSION

A skillful listener is much more than a passive receiver of information. Like a conductor who silently directs musicians to play the notes in the proper sequence, the accomplished listener has the power to orchestrate a conversation through masterful use of pauses and silences. He creates the responses he wants to hear by presenting irresistible opportunities to express them; he allows the other person to talk *himself* out of his objections.

Silence can even be aggressive. Over the phone, a pause in the conversation strikes many as "dead air" that must be filled. Experienced employment interviewers often capitalize on this fact by remaining silent when the candidate finishes speaking, knowing that the disconcerted applicant may well blurt out a revealing statement: "Actually, I was fired."

Your pauses can be equally provocative. After the other speaker appears to conclude his thoughts, wait several beats to pick up the conversation. Often his last-minute statements will prove the most illuminating: The stress of silence may spur him to express thoughts he'd previously censored. Or he may present a valuable clue to his needs or desires as an offhand remark, in an attempt to disguise its true importance.

When you're speaking, appropriately positioned pauses can help structure the other person's responses. A dramatic pause after a statement invites the listener to voice his comments or questions while they're fresh in his mind.

Since you won't want to draw premature objections, place these encouraging silences after your strong points to promote agreement; or after interesting but complex ideas that you're about to elaborate upon. If a question does emerge, you'll already have a fluent response prepared.

Pauses in the *middle* of a sentence, on the other hand, compel attention to key elements of your presentation. A suspenseful pause before the exciting message startles the listener into alertness, while a pause after it gives its import more time to register with the listener. And since you're still in the middle of a thought you've effectively choked off untimely interruptions or comments.

Here's how I might use the technique to pitch a client's book to a publisher: "Nancy, this novel is a . . . [suspenseful pause] . . . psychosexual thriller where the serial killer is . . . [pause] . . . a beautiful woman who murders . . . [pause] . . . the rich and powerful and a detective who must decide . . . [pause] . . . whether to betray . . . [pause] . . . his job or the woman he loves."

To use pauses effectively, the right timing is crucial: The pause must be long enough to capture interest, but short enough to prevent any impression that you've lost the thread of your ideas. A slow count of five is ideal, although you may find yourself so used to a rapid-fire delivery that you're initially uncomfortable introducing even such a brief delay. With practice, however, you will soon perfect the use of intentional pauses.

ASKING THE RIGHT QUESTIONS

While a judiciously placed pause encourages response, a direct question demands it. However, posing a question has its dangers: By promoting reflection on your ideas, you could be prompting the other person to start thinking critically. To circumvent this hazard, both the timing and wording of questions must often be designed to limit the range of responses to those most helpful to your cause.

Most questions fall into five basic categories, each of which has a distinctive role in your conversational repertoire. Here's a look at how and when to employ each type:

Qualifying questions: In the early part of a conversation it's often desirable to assay whether there's a profitable basis for further discussion. Here the purpose isn't to control or guide responses, but to probe in a straightforward manner for relevant information: "Are you ready to discuss price?" "Who would be making the final decision on this matter?" "When would be the earliest date of completion?"

If the objective is to qualify a potential customer before making a sales presentation, you may prefer to word your questions so as to make negative responses more difficult. Rather than say, "Do you use temporary office help?" for example, a better wording would be, "How often do you use temporary office help?" Although it's still possible to respond "Never," the expanded spectrum of possible answers is now shaded toward eliciting more encouraging replies.

What if your qualifying questions evoke an ambivalent or negative response? If the reply convinces you that the call would be unproductive, you've still identified one of the other person's hot buttons that might be used to advantage on another occasion. Or careful listening to such statements as, "No, because . . . [objection]" or "Yes, but . . . [objection]" may reveal that it's in your power to turn around this attitude.

Leading questions: Another effective way of using questions early in the discussion is to present concepts the other person is virtually certain to agree with and build upon these points in later discussion. If, for example, the objective was to establish a favorable climate for negotiation, you might ask, "Did you get the sense from last week's trade journal cover story that this kind of property is getting hotter every day?" or "How would you like a one-week exclusive on this project before we put it out for general auction?"

Presumptive questions: Once you've created points of agreement through leading questions, you can then encourage the respondent to go a step further by posing questions that presuppose the positive result: "Since we agree that the right marketing would be the key to putting a project like this across, do you think that radio spots or print ads would be the way to go?"

By directing discussion to an exploration of options, the respondent is enticed into temporarily imagining your plan or deal as a reality. She's cast into the flattering role of expert, and with a bit of encouragement may now begin selling herself on the idea that what you propose is doable. However, this approach must be coupled with attentive listening for signs of resistance: There's a definite line between guiding and bulldozing.

Nondirective questions: A question of this type has become the trademark of New York Mayor Ed Koch, who frequently inquires of constituents, "How am I doing?" Koch's request for feedback places no limits on the respondents's replies: They could equally well say, "You're the worst mayor since Boss Tweed," or "I count you among my blessings every night."

Koch's question—and such similar queries as, "How does the plan strike you so far?" or "What do you think?"—represent a high stakes play where delivery is crucial to achieving the desired effect. A hint of trepidation in your tone suggests that you harbor secret doubts, while a voice full of cheerful expectation displays a disarming vulnerability. It implies that you're brave enough to risk being punctured with deflating remarks but confident in your powers of persuasion.

Questions to confirm or clarify: Since unclear wording or an unfamiliar concept can confuse even the most careful listener, it's important to test your understanding of what's been said from time to time. One easy way to do this is to paraphrase what you have just heard: "So you think we should investigate whether overseas manufacture would reduce the unit cost?" The speaker can then correct misunderstandings or add further details.

You may find yourself reluctant to expose any holes in your knowledge by asking for definitions or clarifications of new terms or concepts. However, your curiosity and desire to learn will often make a positive impression: The other person is likely to enjoy sharing his expertise with you. And since words can have different implications to different people, a quick query now could prevent expensive or embarrassing misunderstandings later.

Interjecting factual questions is also a tactful way to pin down the glib speaker who's trying to breeze by on generalities. Make sure you've determined what news reporters call "the five W's"—who, what, where, when and why: "What provision have you made for late delivery, and who will bear any resulting costs?"

RESPONSIVE LISTENING

Now that you've got him talking, how do you let him know that you're listening avidly? On the telephone, your total silence may spark concern that you're not paying attention or that there's a poor connection. To show understanding and interest, deftly give encouraging comments that don't break the other person's flow: "I see," "Yes," "Good point" or "Interesting."

Such comments should be used frequently enough to convey the idea that he's reaching an appreciative audience, but sparingly enough to avoid the impression that you're trying to hustle him along faster. Usually a comment after every third sentence is sufficient. When you'd like the speaker to elaborate on one of his statements, try the psychoanalytic technique of repeating his last phrase in a thoughtful tone.

What if the speaker has disgressed into irrelevancies or has launched into a long-winded monologue? Here's your cue to slide adroitly back into the conversation with a discreet interruption: "That's an excellent point, and precisely why . . ." Then steer the conversation diplomatically back to the business at hand.

CONVERSATIONAL RED FLAGS

Now that you've encouraged the speaker to address matters that interest you and offered yourself as an agreeable audience, what should you be listening for? Words can be interpreted in several ways: They could be a straightforward statement, a misdirection to conceal an underlying need or motivation, an attempt to manipulate you or an outright lie.

The way speakers choose to structure their sentences and the frequency with which they use certain parts of speech can reveal quite a bit about personality, according to Dr. Walter Weintraub, professor of psychiatry at the University of Maryland School of Medicine, who's written a book on verbal behavior. Here's a look at some common phrases that may be psychologically significant:

"By the way . . ." Although this phrase is designed to create the illusion of a casual or spontaneous thought that's just struck the speaker, more often than not it's a preface for a message that is actually quite important to the speaker. A similar import is conveyed by "Before I forget." Both phrases are especially significant when used near the end of the conversation or when the stated purpose has apparently been

accomplished, since the speaker will anticipate that you'll have
let your guard down at these points.

"To be perfectly honest . . ." When the speaker uses such
words as "frankly," "honestly," "to tell the truth," odds are that
he's protesting a bit *too* much. Professions of honesty usually
signal either that the speaker is being deceptive or that he's
defensive about some implication of suspicion on your part.

Perhaps the ultimate example of this speaking pattern can
be heard on the Watergate tapes when former President Ri-
chard Nixon says: "The report was not frankly accurate. Well it
was accurate but it was not full. And he tells me that the reason
it was not full, was that he didn't know. Whether that is true or
not, I don't know. Although it wasn't, I'm told. But I'm satisfied
with it."

"Of course . . ." "Naturally . . ." Here's an attempt to slide
something by you by presenting it as a given: "Of course we'll
retain exclusive merchandising rights." Another frequent use
of these phrases is to convey an element of doubt or deceit: "Of
course I have no intention of retaining another agent" would
probably translate as "I'm seeing the other fellow later this
afternoon, but I probably won't fire you until tomorrow morning."

"Because," "since" and "in order to." Heavy use of these
"explainer" words may indicate a predisposition for excessive
rationalization, according to Dr. Weintraub. Intriguingly, an
extreme reliance on these terms usually signals a distorted
view of reality: Dr. Weintraub has found that they crop up
frequently in the speech of hospitalized psychiatric patients
suffering from symptoms of paranoia.

"Kind of" and *"what you might call."* These are essentially terms of indecision, since the speaker is usually qualifying what he or she says in order to avoid making a verbal commitment or to escape the responsibility of a definite pronouncement.

"But," "although," "nevertheless." These verbal constructions tend to be overused by impulsive individuals who are likely to leap into decisions then reverse themselves when it comes time to take action. The speaker talks himself or herself in and out of a position easily, making it hard for you to pin down an absolute commitment.

"Who, me?" One noted British barrister has found that the most reliable means of assaying the guilt or innocence of a client he's defending is to ask him bluntly if he committed the crime. If the client reponds with a direct denial, he's usually innocent (or an extremely accomplished liar), while the overwhelming majority of the guilty will attempt to evade the amount of untruth by posing a question of their own.

"Let's keep in touch." Often used as a polite brush-off when the speaker wants to avoid the bluntness of a direct refusal. It can also be a neutral phrase to signal that the speaker considers the call completed and would like to hang up.

"Trust me." The most suspect phrase of all, this probably translates to "If you shake hands with me, better count your fingers afterwards."

REVEALING HIDDEN RESERVATIONS

Suppose your listening strategies result in the speaker's voicing an objection. Does this signal failure? Not at all; often the most productive dialog occurs after the speaker has brought negative reactions out into the open where they can be defused, rather than leaving them to smolder in the back of his or her mind.

To improve your ability to listen to objections effectively, it helps to view them as requests for additional information, not personal rejections. After all, if the speaker was absolutely uninterested would she bother to explain her thinking when there are so many easy ways to end an unwelcome call? What she may really be saying is, "I haven't bought your story—yet."

Listening carefully to the exact wording of the negative comments is the first step. Show her that you understand and empathize with the objection by repeating it back to her: "The problem is the scheduling, am I right?" This neutral statement both disarms any hostility behind the objection and affords an opportunity to expand upon or clarify the concern.

Next, probe for other unstated objections by crystallizing the concern into an affirmative statement: "Since price seems to be the obstacle here, I take it you'd be quite interested if a more attractive budget could be put together." Pause long enough to get a response. If the speaker agrees, you've made progress by obtaining an indirect commitment to limit disagreement to this particular point.

Since some speakers raise false objections to direct you away from their true motives, a low-keyed request for a commitment based on your removing the objection either confirms that the real complaint has already been revealed or extracts a new description of the problem, which can be tested in the same manner: "If I help you overcome these reservations [list each one], then would you be interested?"

While you may now be tempted to systematically debate each objection in turn, resist the impulse. A forceful tone may enable you to "win" the conversation—but not to effect any real change in the other's attitude. Responsive listening, on the other hand, can actually enable you to win over the other person by providing an unemotional forum for him to present and discuss his concerns.

Since most of us anticipate an immediate counterattack when we voice a negative sentiment, the speaker may take a defensive tone as she presents objections. *Agreeing* with her is an unexpected and therefore effective counter that will discharge much of the tension: "I think your concern about cost is an important point, and I'm glad you brought it up."

Once resistance has been softened by mild words like these, you're in a good position to show why the apparent objection is actually a point in your favor. (Chapter Seven will dissect some common sales objections and offer effective counterarguments to them.)

THE ULTIMATE TEST

While a sharp ear for the subtleties of others' speech is crucial to telephone effectiveness, developing your ability to listen to *yourself* can be more profitable still. Only by hearing yourself exactly as others hear you can you be completely confident that you're exploiting your communication skills to the fullest—with masterful use of silence *and* speech.

The tape recorder can be a potent—although disconcerting—tool for self-analysis. You may wish to tape a few typical calls (check with the phone company for current regulations first), or enlist a friend for a bit of role-playing in which the two of you act out some of your customary telephone transactions. It's likely that you'll be surprised—and perhaps shocked—by what you hear.

Most startling, if you haven't taped yourself before, is the unfamiliar sound of your own voice. The sounds you're accustomed to hearing issue from your mouth are actually the distortions of bone conduction. What others hear are the vibrations produced by movements of your larynx; what you hear are these sounds plus other, internal vibrations that are resonating through your skull and jaw. (Tips on getting in better voice can be found in Chapter Five, if you detect any deficiencies.)

Once you've adjusted to your undistorted voice, try casting yourself in the role of audience. Is your message consistently conveying the sort of professional image you're striving for? Do your words have the ring of conviction and confidence? And what about your listening skills? Do you allow the other person plenty of speaking room and hear him out before replying?

Odds are that you'll find both qualities to applaud and some bad habits you'd rather edit out of your next phone performance. Once your ear is tuned to these high and low notes, you'll also begin to hear your eloquence increasing. By rehearsing with the tape and consciously applying these lessons to your future calls, you may ultimately find yourself listening to the sweet sound of success—your winning telephone style!

4

POWER PHONING

For a call with real clout, it's hard to match the impact of the world's first call, made on March 10, 1876. About to test a new transmitter, Alexander Graham Bell had sent his assistant to another room to await the test message. Accidentally spilling some battery acid on his clothes, the phone's inventor anxiously cried out, "Mr. Watson, come here. I want you!" Watson, more dazzled by the unique delivery of the summons than its urgency, rushed into the room yelling, "Mr. Bell, I heard every word you said—distinctly!"

Having a burning desire to communicate (as Bell did, quite literally) isn't enough to turn a call into a dramatic event in the modern world. The average person is summoned to the phone upward of 1,500 times a year—and probably regards most of his telephone traffic as another variety of noise pollution. Though your audience is somewhat jaded, they still secretly hunger for mystery, adventure, and magical surprise. Creating verbal pyrotechnics is easier than you may imagine: What you'll need is to cultivate a sense of *showmanship*.

SMOKE AND MIRRORS

Not only will a little artful drama make speaking with you more exciting to others, but it's a potent weapon in deflecting the parries of the power players you'll inevitably encounter on the phone. Such opponents usually script their dialog so as to cast you as a bit player while they assume the leading role in their psychodrama of intimidation and power. With a command of telephone theatrics, you can *upstage* such acts of aggression—while scoring telephone triumphs of your own.

A great moment in phone history must have been the duel of wits between legendary Hollywood showman Mike Todd and a fellow producer. Irritated by Todd's simple but devastatingly effective ploy of grandly announcing that he was calling from his car, the rival counterattacked during his next call. After reaching Todd in his car, the rival opened with, "Mike, I'm calling from my Rolls," aware that Todd's was the less impressive car. Without missing a beat, Todd rejoined, "Hold on, I'm speaking on my *other* line."

What's the best way to counter such ploys? The obvious—but not always best—route to one-upmanship is escalation, and the possible tactics are almost endless. Perhaps appropriately, the U.S. Pentagon seems to have achieved true telephonic overkill: Its 25,000-line switchboard is the world's largest, as must be its annual phone bill of $8.7 million. The presidential retreat, Camp David, offers a unique degree of calling convenience with phones strategically mounted every few yards in the trees lining its rustic walks.

Then there's the Rolodex play favored by many would-be power players. The point is to impale as many names as possible on its prongs, then create a second, smaller wheel of fortune containing the secret unlisted numbers of the truly important. The owner of the Rolodex can then turn her cards to trumps by letting visitors "accidentally" observe one of the hot Washington numbers that she presumably calls constantly.

A magnificent array of smoke and mirrors, however, doesn't always ensure a successful illusion. Consider the case of a minor political candidate who outfitted his private plane with high tech telephones, expecting an inundation of calls from eager reporters and contributors. When the bell failed to toll, he resorted to the rather desperate tactic of mailing out engraved announcements of his plane's phone number—ingeniously presented as a memorable seven-letter word. Finally he did make a profitable connection—a status-conscious sheik telephoned an offer to buy the plane, which the now disillusioned politician accepted.

Power props work best as visible reminders of their owner's actual achievements, rather than as symbols hinting at his future aspirations. As a fledgling power player, the politician erred by exposing his delusions of grandeur too vividly, making himself a tempting target for putdowns from the really powerful (the most devastating of which, of course, was simply not to call). He'd have done much better with the opposite approach: sculpting an image of exquisite simplicity.

REVERSE PSYCHOLOGY

As a telephone tactic, reverse psychology offers two advantages that standard success strategies lack. First, it's the *unexpected* move and therefore catches the opposition off guard. Before the other person quite realizes what's hit him, he finds that his apparent strengths have become cumbersome liabilities. Second, it's easy to put into practice: No elaborate equipment or complicated ploys are required. In fact, the whole power of the concept is in its utter simplicity: *Instead of trying to beat the other player at his own game, you win by changing the rules*.

Where the producer who wished to one-up Mike Todd went wrong was by accepting the basic premise that a car phone confers status on its owner. With this assumption, his only possible counter was to try to suggest that he had something even better—a similar phone in his Rolls Royce. If he'd understood reverse psychology, however, he could have neatly turned around the situation in this manner:

Todd: I wanted to catch you before the meeting, so I'm calling from the car.
   Rival: What?
   Todd (louder, but less confident): It's Mike Todd.
   Rival (deliberately speaking almost inaudibly): We've got a terrible connection, Mike.
   Todd (louder still): I'm in the Mercedes.
   Rival (very loudly): So that's the problem.
   Todd (switching tactics): Hold on, there's a call coming in on the other line.
   Rival promptly hangs up and pretends to have been disconnected when Todd calls back.
   Todd: What happened?
   Rival: My nephew used to have the same trouble when he was driving a radio cab. I've heard it's caused by sunspots.

These thrusts from the rival producer have the effect of all reverse psychology ploys: They make the would-be power player sense that something has inexplicably gone wrong. Todd now feels that as a gentleman he owes the other producer an apology for subjecting him to his malfunctioning status symbol; and more humiliating still, realizing that the rival views his fancy car phone in the same category as the equipment used by cab drivers. And then there's the sunspot remark: Todd feels obscurely troubled by the idea, even though he half suspects that the rival just invented it.

While the usual power approach is to inflate one's importance, the reverse psychologist punctures other's pretensions by his tremendous ordinariness. Done correctly, this tactic conveys the impression that you are so secure in your status that you can afford to downplay it. To avoid the potential danger of seeming believably ordinary, you must throw in enough showmanship to seem *extravagantly* ordinary, like the British aristocrats who modestly choose not to be known by their hereditary titles.

The editor-in-chief of one of New York's most prestigious literary publishers seems to have mastered this delicate balance. When one of his authors called recently, elaborately describing her latest opus as "an intricate play of point and counterpoint, which symbolically centers on the theme of revenge," his laconic response was: "It ain't for us." (His other stock reply, for books he liked, was: "Send the sucker over.")

Compare this result with that of the typical success stunt. Let's say the editor-in-chief took the call on his speaker phone, which has the effect of making both parties sound as if they are shouting into tin cans. Then, just when the novelist was at a high point in her presentation, she was abruptly interrupted by an unannounced third party, a confederate of the editor-in-chief, saying something like, "A bit recherché, *nicht wahr?*"

After being insulted in three languages (one of which she doesn't understand) by an unknown individual who may have nothing to do with editorial decisions, the novelist would probably be more defensive than deflated. Her next move, very likely, would be to hotly debate the point with new rhetorical flourishes. In the first example, however, she is left speechless and filled with a grudging admiration. Being so cheerfully lowbrow, she reasons, can only be a sign of the most discerning literary taste.

ARRESTING THE USUAL SUSPECTS

How do you apply the unexpected reversal to standard power approaches? Here's a guide to identifying the opposition's style and countering it:

The Aristocrat: In *Jane Trahey on Women and Power,* the author describes receiving a typical aristocratic putdown when she read her employer, Herbert Marcus, Sr., some advertising copy she'd written about a "sensational" fur sale at Neiman-Marcus. The store owner's response was: "Miss Trahey, the word 'sensational' is a word that I have always reserved for the Immaculate Conception. A person who would use a word like 'sensational' is not, I think, a person who was born to the purple."

While most elitists are a bit more subtle, their scoring tactics exploit similar social distinctions: The unstated message is that your language or lifestyle marks you as not quite a gentleman or less than ladylike. But even if you lack a purple image, there's no need to let yourself be outclassed. Most of these aristocrats are a bit ersatz themselves—a point you can easily make through use of reverse psychology. Trahey, for example, could have turned the tables on the department store tycoon by replying, "Quite true—otherwise I wouldn't have gone into trade. Now I hope I'm vulgar enough to get really *rich.*"

What about the opposite approach—cultivating a class act of your own? The trouble with social-climbing is that guarding against the slight slips that expose your true status takes real effort. Furthermore, even if you do it right, you've only achieved parity with the purple-born. With a deliberately downscale style, however, you can't lose. If you are read as a genuine Horatio Alger story, even slight success on your part becomes dramatic and admirable. Any suspicion that you're scamming him, on the other hand, forces the opponent to wonder if your true status is so high that you can appreciate the fun of slumming.

The Terrorist: There's nothing refined about this character: He's shamelessly melodramatic, full of bluster and brazen tricks and legendary for his hair-trigger temper. His absurd degree of chutzpah fortunately is tempered with just enough charm to quell the murderous wrath his despotic behavior might otherwise provoke in you. The real reason you continue to deal with him, however, is that he's gained sufficient authority to toss a few goodies your way—you just wish you could get the rewards without the rigmarole.

Since the terrorist likes to launch a call with a preemptive strike, startle him with an unexpected retreat. Let's say he tries the irritating ploy of having his secretary feint her way past yours, claiming that Mr. Terrorist "is on the line." When you pick up the phone, you immediately realize that once again you've been fooled into speaking to Mr. T's secretary, who now instructs you to hold until her boss deigns to speak with you. This rudeness can best be countered with exquisite courtesy: You immediately *apologize to the secretary* for having answered the phone at an inconvenient moment, and hang up before Mr. T can get on the line.

At this point Mr. T may be one down, but he's hardly out of the contest. Having failed to draw first blood with his secretary strategy, he'll reach into his limited repertoire of tactics and decide upon a frontal assault: a loud, angry tirade about some petty grievance he's harboring. Other than a chuckle or two at some of his more vivid phrases, remain completely silent until the sound and fury have died away. Now that most of the fight's gone out of him, you've reached the right psychological moment to call his bluff (if yours is the superior position) or to wear him down by repeating the same reasonable response in a soft and hypnotic voice until he gives up.

The Technocrat: Unlike the average layperson who can barely decode such basic computer acronyms as RAM, ROM, and CPU, this opponent claims intimacy with "trojan horses," "64K motherboards" and "CompuSex." Through his command of computerbabble, he's able to make unintelligible and vaguely intimidating remarks even when a no-tech topic is under discussion. Here's a typical example of the Technocrat in action:

> *Layperson* (winding up what she considers a telling point): "So we'll actually realize a six percent savings in the first month . . ."
>
> *Technocrat* (almost under his breath): Gigo.
>
> *Layperson* (wondering if she misunderstood): Gigo?
>
> *Technocrat* (laughing slightly): Did I say 'gigo'? I'm sorry—I meant to say 'lifo.'
>
> *Layperson* (still wondering what significance, if any, "gigo" has): Lifo?
>
> *Technocrat:* Bit of computer jargon for what you were saying. L-I-F-O—Last In, First Out. But do go on.

While the best way to counter the "gigo gambit" and other high tech tactics is to become computer literate yourself—more easily done than you might suspect—reverse psychology offers a more immediate solution. At the first mention of a computer term, confess your complete ignorance of electronics and ask eagerly for tips on reprogramming your secretary's "intelligent" typewriter so it will cease spewing out question marks whenever she strikes the umlaut key.

The Millionaire: Although her riches are obviously *nouveau,* it's still grating to hear the constant chink of the cash register in such statements as, "We've been house-hunting in Connecticut, but it's impossible to find anything decent in the million-dollar range anymore. Of course we could always sell the summer house, but . . ."

The answer here is to adopt the tactics of the Old Money, who never discuss price and are unabashedly stingy anyway. Devalue her references to expensive activities by offering a downscale equivalent: While she's idling at some fashionable watering spot, you're teaching the children how to clam at the public beach. Your tone should imply that you secretly rate yours as the more amusing activity but are too tactful to say so.

Once you have the basic approach, try a few refinements, such as references to inexpensive but esoteric hobbies: "I'll be out all night with my telescope, watching the moon cross the earth's ecliptic." (No need to mention that this event occurs twice every month.) Another variation is to capture the moral high ground with the "noblesse oblige" ploy: "I wish I could get away. But with the shelter for homeless children so close to completion . . ."

The Name-Dropper: You'll recognize him by his penchant for sprinkling the conversation with frequent references to the close encounters he's had with the famous, the rich and the notorious. Fortunately, it's easy to score off those who play the fame game. If he mentions lesser luminaries or TV stars of any degree of celebrity, profess bewilderment: "Vanna White? Is she the new marketing director at Warner's?" You can then appear both amused and amazed as the name-dropper explains, and then cap his comments by saying, "Absolutely delightful—hearing this almost makes me wish I had a television set."

Superstars of the past can be addressed with either of these remarks: "Good old X, is he still alive?" or "I just saw her name in the *Times* crossword puzzle the other day." But what of those megacelebrities who are impossible to dismiss? A good remark is, "He's shorter than he looks, isn't he?" Change the subject quickly as the opponent wrestles with the convoluted logic of this.

The Intellectual: What if you're confronted with one of those intimidating arty types who converses knowledgeably about obscure Latin American poets, Jungian psychology, arcane political issues, the Tao of physics, abstract expressionism and other esoterica? Though your impulse may be to seize upon one of the phone's ready-made escapes, such as claiming that you have to take a call from Istanbul, a more disconcerting move is to remark thoughtfully, "Oh, I don't know."

Once you've broken the flow, there are a variety of gambits to try. You can fluster the opponent with irrelevant facts (either real or invented). In a discussion of theater, for example, you might remark that the word "set" has 194 definitions. Quibble with definitions: "But surely you mean *neo*-Jungian?" Repeat one of his more obvious statements in a hollow, dogmatic tone, as if to show agreement. Offer meaningless criticism: "I'm sorry, but to me he seems like a Coca-Cola journalist." Or be unembarrassedly plebeian: "I've always had a taste for really *good* trash."

The Expert: Is it possible to bluff your way past that supreme intimidator, the expert? Emphatically yes; why most of us are so easily dazzled by experts is that we fail to realize that their twenty-four-karat credentials will usually prove to be mere electroplate upon closer scrutiny. Even the unquestionable authority, however, has his Achilles' heel: an unwillingness to be found ignorant in *any* area. By enticing him outside the confines of his expertise and catching him in some imprudent pronouncement, you can puncture his credibility while establishing yourself as a counterexpert.

The bolder move, of course, is to tackle the expert on his or her home ground. Since a little knowledge can be dangerous when the opponent is an expert, psychological warfare works better than fortifying yourself with facts. Defuse his standard weaponry—sober recitations of studies, statistics and charts that support his statements—by exposing the psychological weakness of this approach: It lacks fun, play and sex appeal. Imply that as he's poring over economic indicators and scanning charts for "dormant bottoms" and "necklines," you have the financial equivalent of perfect pitch—an *intuitive* sense of market feel.

An amusing variation on presenting yourself as a devil-may-care type is to occasionally tell anecdotes about antics of some madcap third party, who may be either real or invented. Each of this colorful character's adventures should have a common theme: how he recklessly flouted the conventional wisdom and won. Your expert will gradually feel an irrational desire to abandon logic and enter the seductive realm of hunches and luck. Once you've gotten him playing this game, the expert's defeat is assured.

5

AVOIDING TELEPHONE HANG-UPS

"Buy that voice!" said a Hollywood movie mogul to one of his underlings. He had been captivated by the voice of a young, unknown actress who was speaking on the radio.

While few of us have voices that high-powered executives would want to buy, an attractive presentation and delivery of your ideas could make important people want to buy *from* you. Sounding like a winner—with confident speech and a professional manner—also pays off in your other telephone transactions: Less of your energy and time will be frittered away though inefficiency and delays created by others, and more will be spent on those profitable connections that advance your career.

A MILLION-DOLLAR ATTITUDE

The first key to strong communication skills is a strong self-image. Consider the telephone salesperson who was frustrated because he'd never sold a million-dollar life insurance policy to anyone. When he complained of this failure to his wife, she said, "Who'd want to spend so much? After all, you make a good income, and you only carry a hundred thousand dollars' worth." Suddenly the problem became clear to him: The next morning he wrote up his first million-dollar sale—to *himself*.

What that salesman bought was an attitude: By knowing that he was literally worth a million, he acquired a sense of inner worth that enabled him to speak with conviction to his prospects. Most of us could benefit from making a similar sale to ourselves, not by investing in insurance, but by selling ourselves the confidence that we've got something worthwhile to say.

Too many of us approach the telephone with trepidation. Take Paul, for example. He's well educated, bright, hard-working and attractive—seemingly the ideal candidate for success. Yet he's been remained mired in the same low-level job at an import/export firm for the past five years. The reports of his superiors are always the same: "Paul is a good worker and an excellent thinker, but he displays insufficient initiative and takes too long getting things done."

What they mean is that Paul would rather write a letter than make a telephone call, even when it is abundantly evident that the solution, to the problem is quite literally at his fingertips—a simple phone call away.

While Paul's phonophobia is a chronic problem, most of us have experienced flickers of telephone shyness on occasion—sometimes with good reason. A young stockbroker I know advised a client to invest $20,000 in speculative stock that was being touted as the next IBM. No sooner was the purchase made than the stock headed south and the investment sunk to a mere $4,500. The broker knew he should call the client immediately, but couldn't bring himself to do it. Instead, he lost sleep and appetite and couldn't focus on his work. Finally, he made the dreaded call. The client cut through his apologies and said, "Young man, I can take bad news, but I do like it to be *news*, not ancient history."

While some people defer unpleasant calls, others face their telephone transactions with the conviction that something is sure to go wrong—and the prophecy becomes self-fulfilling. The call goes awry, reinforcing the phonophobe's underlying assumption that the phone is an unappealing method of communication. Actually, it is the *fear* that's the problem, not the phone.

Similar insecurities are reflected in the opposite problem— telephonitis, an adult version of separation anxiety that makes it difficult to end calls with dispatch. Good salespeople know that there's a "magic moment" in a call, when the other person is ready to buy or act or has irrevocably decided not to do so. Knowing when this precise point has been reached is central to profitable phoning: If the answer is yes, the deal is made; if it's not, a further investment of time is useless and may arouse resentment.

To overcome these common psychological hang-ups, try a few tactics from that most insecure of professions, acting. They'll help you fake the confidence you need for those difficult calls. Best of all, your act may prove so successful that you find that you too believe. Here's how:

• **Start with a good script.** A common cause of both excessive talk and telephone timidity is being unsure of what you want to say. Organize a list of points to cover, assemble all necessary files and facts and mentally rehearse the conversation. Do you anticipate objections or complaints? Script yourself good lines to address these problems, and both your conversational fluency and sense of conviction will rise.

• **Imagine yourself succeeding.** Both actors and athletes know the importance of psyching yourself up before performing. A good method is to visualize yourself in action: lifting the receiver, dialing the number, leaning back in your chair and beginning to speak. Watch yourself, in your mind's eye, make the gestures and facial expressions you associate with confidence and authority. These thoughts, say trainers, will send appropriate messages to your muscles, and these physical sensations will spark related emotions.

• **Get physical on the phone.** Using body language *during* your call, though not visible to the other person, will enhance your voice appeal. Gestures and expressions help you speak more effectively in person, and the same power can be conveyed through your voice. You'll be more involved in your words, so your ability to deliver a convincing message will be strengthened.

• **Pull your emotional strings.** To add extra fire to your words, look for a psychological "trigger." Actors often conjure up some incident from the past where they felt the desired emotion and channel that feeling into the scene ahead. Try to vividly recall some of your previous telephone triumphs or other business successes to get yourself in the proper mood.

• **Create a winning vision.** To make your ideas sound more real to the other person, let them come to life in your mind. Studies show that successful people are adept at inspiring themselves via fantasy. Imagine the plan, project or idea in action. Summoning up as many concrete details as possible will help you to dramatize the presentation and share your vision with others.

• **Play to the audience.** Even though you may have never seen the other speaker in person, visualizing your audience and his or her physical surroundings will help you project your personality better. It's easy to get lost in the cocoon of your own thoughts on the phone, so reaching out with your imagination will let you make stronger contact with the person on the other end.

GETTING IN GOOD VOICE

A distinctive, agreeable telephone voice is a valuable asset in both business and social communication. It can characterize you positively to new associates, set the right tone for effective communication and add life and drama to your words. To those who only know you by telephone, it's a vital element of their image of you. To let them hear the sweet sound of success in your voice, try these speaking strategies:

Get loose. Before exercising your voice, warm it up with a few relaxing techniques. Humming loosens the tongue muscles, helping you to project positive vocal qualities. Spend a few seconds humming in high and low pitches. Now, relax your mouth. Most of us speak without much movement of the lips and jaw, but our voices would sound richer and stronger if we merely opened our mouths a little wider. This relaxes the vocal cords and provides more room for resonance.

Defuse additional tension by deep diaphragmatic breathing. The right breathing habits support good voice quality while reducing the strain on your vocal apparatus. Practice filling and emptying your lungs completely by taking quick, short sniffs of air through your nose, as you feel your chest expand. When you are full, say, "Ho! Ho! Ho!" releasing air until you can no longer speak. Then sit up straight, which increases lung volume, and breathe deeply in and out a few times.

A fews yawns are also a good way to loosen up. When a Japanese manufacturer introduced fifteen-second yawn breaks several times a work shift, productivity on the assembly line rose dramatically. You can enjoy similar benefits to your speaking efficiency—speech therapists say that tension may be the worst opponent to acquiring an attractive voice. Another good tactic is the "body scan," in which you rapidly check each part of your body for tension, and systematically relax it.

Watch pacing. Despite the negative connotations of a fast talking style, most of us do speak overly rapidly on the phone, which can cause important ideas to glide past the listener's ear without registering effectively. To determine if you're speaking at the optimal pace, time yourself reading seven hundred words of text. If it took you five minutes, your speech is average; if the time was significantly lower, your pace is too rapid. Practice with a stop watch helps you achieve the correct rate.

Speaking quickly is often associated with another poor speech habit: impulsively responding before we've fully thought out our words. This can lead to accidentally offending the listener or making a weak point that undermines your previous thoughts. You may also give the sense you're unsure or don't know what you are talking about. A mental deep breath before speaking adds emphasis to what you say and lets you censor poorly formed ideas.

Slow speech can inspire confidence. The listener perceives that the words reflect measured, well-thought-out ideas. It's particularly effective to slow down when you get to important concepts, since the increased pauses between words give each one greater weight with the listener. But don't drag *everything* out excessively, or you'll lose suspense. Variation—sometimes fast and hot, sometimes slow and deliberate—adds interest and a touch of showmanship to your speech.

Reflecting the pace of the *other* speaker can be a good means of establishing rapport. Fast talkers can become impatient with very slow speech; while slow speakers may feel that a more rapid speaker is trying to put something over on them. Either way a bad impression may result. That's why it's important to have range and flexibility in your speaking style—a minor adjustment could make a major difference in how you're perceived.

Control volume. Do people frequently ask you to speak up or say that they're having trouble with their phone? If so, you may be speaking too softly. While a soft voice can be seductive in a social call, a strong voice definitely carries more authority in business phoning. A weak or whispering voice suggests an image of meekness or of having something to hide—messages you don't want to transmit to the listener.

Being too loud is another common telephone fault—we've all encountered the screamer who acts as though telephone transmission was solely a matter of lung power. Since associates may hesitate to tell you that you speak too loudly, you may want to check with a friend or spouse if you suspect that you are guilty of this. A loud voice can also signal a degree of hearing loss, which should be investigated medically.

Varying your volume is probably the most dramatic way to make a point on the phone. A sudden drop in your volume can be used to suggest that you are about to pass along some exciting confidences or a hot secret you know, while turning up the volume might imply, depending on context, sudden enthusiasm for an idea, a decision to act, an unequivocal refusal or anger.

A winning pitch. Are you speaking at your correct pitch? Few of us do, maintains speech pathologist Evelyn Burge Bowling, the author of *Voice Power*. Her suggestion is: "To determine your natural pitch, take a deep breath exactly as you do when yawning and say aloud, 'Ahhh . . . I know that.' " Once you've located your best pitch, establish it as a speaking habit with daily practice.

The best way to perfect your pitch, says Bowling, is to yawn or sigh, say, "Ahh . . ." then follow with everyday phrases from your normal speaking vocabulary, such as, "I am calling you to say . . ." or "My extension is . . ." A week or two of this exercise is usually enough to establish the habit; however, you may find at first that you slip back into the old pitch under stress. Further effort should eliminate this problem as well.

Speak clearly. Since it's especially easy to be misunderstood on the telephone, devote extra attention to your pronunciation, especially when saying the words most dear to the listener's heart: his or her name. Having often heard my own quite common first name, Lisa, rendered as "Liza" or even "Leslie," I empathize with the frustration of the more exotically named whose monikers are mangled constantly. Mastering listeners' names the first time you hear them—perhaps through jotting them down phonetically—gains you their lasting gratitude and immediate rapport.

If your own name is considered difficult by others, the right presentation of it will implant it solidly in the listener's mind. A good way to accomplish this is to use a mnemonic device, such as a word that rhythms with it. It's important to choose the correct word: a woman with the poetically inspired first name of Porphyria would do better suggesting the rhyme of "superior" than "inferior." A similar approach can be used in spelling out the name: You might say, "It's 'i' as in 'iconoclast' and 's' as in 'sophisticated,' " thus associating those two qualities with your image.

Eliminate verbal tics. While an instantly recognizable voice can contribute to a strong phone image, annoying speaking habits can make you memorable in a negative manner. For example, I once had a client with the habit of booming, "Greetings!" at the start of every call. The first time I was amused, by the twentieth call I felt on edge before the conversation had even gotten off the ground. Other irritating habits include constant use of such stalling words as "you know," "well" and "uh"; and flogging some favorite word or phrase to death in every sentence.

A dash of accent. Having a detectable regional accent is *not* a barrier to effective communication. Rather it can be an asset, making acquaintances and associates from your own geographical region feel at home with you, and generating a touch of curiosity and interest among those from elsewhere. Several recent American presidents have had pronounced regional accents, and many other well-known personalities have such distinctive speaking styles that they can be effectively impersonated with a word or two.

If you do wish to diminish a regional accent—perhaps because you've relocated to a different part of the country and want to blend in linguistically—focus on your pronunciation of vowel sounds and the endings of words. Experts say these are usually the primary components of regional variations in speech, and by attacking these you'll make the change most efficiently. You'll also find that, over time, you subconsciously absorb the speech rhythms around you and begin to echo them.

STRENGTHENING YOUR STYLE

By becoming aware of your characteristic speaking patterns, you can improve your speech without sacrificing the uniqueness of your verbal personality. Your natural style is a strength, and forcing drastic changes will only make your words sound insincere and contrived. Instead, your goal should be to master the full potential powers of those special tools—your voice and style of speech. With practice, perhaps by speaking into a tape recorder and watching yourself speak to a mirror, you can learn to express yourself naturally, yet powerfully.

6

"LET ME SPEAK TO THE BOSS, HONEY."

In a vast office whose floor-to-ceiling windows open on a sparkling downtown vista forty stories below, an exquisitely attired vice-president sits behind an enormous expanse of marble desk. On the desk are a dictating machine, a solid gold pen stamped "Cartier" and a chocolate brown phone with several buttons. The telephone rings.

"Hello," says the vice-president.

"Hi, honey," says the voice on the other end of the line. "Let me speak to your boss."

As a female business owner who enjoys answering her own phone, I have frequently found myself the target of telephone chauvinists like this. Although I could have deflected these assaults on my professional status by delegating the task of handling incoming calls to one of my assistants, I decided that a confrontational approach was more compatible with my personality. To the next caller who mistook me for a secretary, I replied sweetly, "Oh, you'd like to speak to a man? Let me connect you with Bob, my assistant."

Since this offer invariably produced a flood of apologies, I like to think that my educational efforts did move a few minds. However, until all such sexual stumbling blocks are eradicated, professional women do need some special telephone techniques to ensure that they receive the respect they deserve.

THE VOICE OF AUTHORITY

How do you increase your calling clout? The first step is to *sound* authoritative. Media expert Muriel Fox, who grooms business men and women for radio and television appearances, believes that women can benefit from a deliberate effort to lower their speaking voices on the telephone. A cute little voice conveys an image of girlishness that undermines the import of your words, while a low voice conveys the ring of command.

Try it yourself. Say, "This is a call of some urgency," in your normal voice, and then repeat the sentence using a slightly lower register. Did you hear a difference? Odds are that your second effort did sound considerably more forceful. Behaviorists maintain that attitudes can follow actions, so that by consciously aiming at an authoritative tone, you can instill yourself with the inner confidence a woman needs to get things done *her* way.

Think it's impossible to change the character of your voice so easily? This true story may convince you otherwise. When a young actress was being tested for her first role, the director admired her acting techniques and striking good looks, but confessed that he was less than enchanted with her squeaky, high-pitched voice. He told her that she could have the role, but that the voice would have to go. Not one to let a high-pitched voice stand between her and stardom, the actress set about to make the change. Through a determined effort and practice, she lowered her voice to a level that the director judged acceptable. The director was John Ford and the actress was Lauren Bacall.

AVOIDING "GIRL TALK"

The second step is to look at your speech patterns. Experts say that the gender of the speaker influences how we'll react to his or her words. The same phrase may signal politeness if the speaker is a man, while conveying indecisiveness if she's a woman. Since studies indicate that male communication patterns register more effectively than the characteristically "feminine" manner or speaking that most women have unconsciously acquired, a few subtle changes in your word choice and phrasing will let you communicate with more authority.

Here's how:

• **Be verbally aggressive.** Men typically use the word "I" more frequently than women, who tend to say "we." Take responsibility for your ideas with strong phrases like: "I've decided . . ." or "My position is . . ." Avoid softening words; rather than saying, "We show a sales increase of about forty percent," assert confidently, "Sales are up forty percent." Two other typically feminine words to eliminate from your speech are "just" and "only," as in: "I just wanted to know if . . ." or "It's only a minor point, but . . ." Tag questions can diminish your effectiveness as well; saying, "I think it's a real money-maker, don't you?" suggests you are insecure about what you say and are asking for approval from the other speaker.

Eliminate from your conversational repertoire any cute phrases; a female associate of mine, for example, has a favorite pejorative term that her male and female colleagues wince upon hearing: The offending word is "pippy-poo." Another equally unfortunate habit is using self-deprecating phrases or humor: One woman I know has an annoying tendency to launch her ideas with such wording as, "In my humble opinion," or "You may think this is a dumb idea, but . . ."

• **Don't let yourself be upstaged.** Study after study proclaims a fact that's long been obvious to women: Men typically interrupt us far more frequently than we interrupt them. But why let them get away with it? Effective tactics include ignoring or dismissing the interruption or courteously confronting the interrupter: "I've anticipated that objection, as you'll see when I have finished describing the plan." Habitual offenders can be deflected before you start by remarks like: "I know you'll have a lot of thoughts on this, so let me run down the five key points before we discuss the details."

Another common male habit is to dominate the conversational stage by speaking loudly. But don't let the dialog degenerate into a shouting match or let yourself be intimidated by his lung power. Instead try a little reverse psychology and speak quietly and firmly, as if to an unruly child. Regain control of the talk with a summation of your own: "You're obviously concerned about the payment schedule; I'll address that now." Then keep talking.

• **Avoid mixed messages.** In a dialog between the sexes, there are a few areas where men and women can get their wires crossed. A typical example is our use of terms of agreement like "uh-huh" and "yes" to encourage the other speaker to expand on his ideas. To a man these verbal nudges imply that you've been sold on his ideas, while your message is only "Tell me more." If you later express disagreement, he may conclude that you're what he considers the typical woman: indecisive and apt to change her mind. To let him know that you're not necessarily buying his story, use neutral comments like: "Go on" or "Let me think about that."

We also have a greater tendency to link our ideas to the

other speaker's last words, which may give a man the illusion
that he's controlling the conversation. Jumping boldly into the
discussion with a new thought can be more strategically sophisticated; he'll respect this approach because it's what he
tends to do. Another potential trouble spot is our willingness to
accept side comments from the other speaker and weave them
into our thoughts. Since he may see this as weakness, take the
male approach to topic control by defining the subject narrowly
and refusing to be diverted by amusing or intriguing tangents.

CONVERSATIONAL MACHISMA

Although your objective is to speak to men in language
they understand and respect, avoid the strategic error of pretending to be "one of the boys." Men have their unfortunate
speech habits too, and acquiring them will only subtract from
your professional image. For example, men frequently use
crude sexual metaphors to describe common business situations; I have often heard them say things like, "I can't get it up
for this deal" or "They're just jerking us off on this." While I
believe that mildly sexy terms add interest to a presentation,
locker room language from a woman can backfire. Not only are
most men better than women at this type of talk, but worse
still, they might interpret it as a sexual come-on from you.

What about the other two approaches to macho conversation: "jock talk" and blood-and-guts expressions? Both of these
can be amusing and vivid elements of your conversational
repertoire if you find them appealing. Being fluent in sports
argot enables you to achieve instant rapport with males who
sprinkle their conversation with terms like "in the ballpark,"
"Monday morning quarterback" and "run interference." An
even more gratifying result is the opportunity to one-up any
males unfortuante enough to be sports illiterate—and you'd be
surprised how many are.

The vernacular of violence is also acceptable business idiom; I was recently amused to hear a female bank trader describing a less-than-satisfactory transaction she'd made in these terms: "Frankly, I got my face ripped off." This kind of bloodthirsty passion for one's work conveys an attractively aggressive quality, as does a direct challenge to a male peer. During a telephone negotiation, for example, you might throw down a conversational gauntlet with a remark like: "I'm going to nail you against the wall on this one; we can't afford any mistakes." Men aren't used to *macha* females, so you'll gain the tactical advantage of surprise.

To give your words additional firepower, try a few military metaphors. If your company will be marketing its new product via phone; tell your listener you'll be *attacking* the market with a *teleblitz*. Other popular expressions include "loose cannon," "poison pill," "smoking gun," "bite the bullet," "corporate brass," "under fire" and "guerrilla tactics." Centuries of cultural imprinting make this sort of speech particularly stirring to the male spirit.

DETECTING THE SECRET SEXIST

Are some men's misconceptions about women and the telephone costing you potential clout? Unfortunately there are plenty of men in the work world who resent, fear or hate women, and try to undermine your power with their phone tactics. While it's easy enough to spot the old-style chauvinist— he's the one who calls you "honey," assumes you're a secretary and treats you with all the respect he'd give a small, not overly bright child—the more dangerous enemy is the secret sexist, who deflates your importance subtly.

Here's how to identify and foil him:

The White Knight: Charm is his secret weapon; he'll use light banter and flattery to direct you away from his key objective—

to deny you the opportunity to accomplish anything of importance. Your efforts to do business become submerged in a morass of social niceties and chivalrous behavior, as he limits his conversation to "women's topics," such as the latest fashions, the weather and inquiries about your husband and children.

The best defense is firmness and a resolutely businesslike tone. Omit all pleasantries from your conversation, even such conventional utterances as, "How are you?" Respond to flattery with icy silence, followed by an abrupt change of topic. Refuse to discuss the weather even if your home has just been demolished by a tornado. And tell him you'd love to chat, but you're busy, busy, busy. That's why you must have his *immediate* answer on this urgent business matter.

The Sneak Thief: His favorite tactic is to cavalierly dismiss most of your suggestions, then rebroadcast them later with a new credit line—*his*. Not only does he raid your brain for ideas that will increase his income and power, but he adds insult to injury, by patronizing you as he does it. He'll imply that your thoughts need the stamp of his approval—even if his status is lower than yours—or that his finishing touches are what turns your raw idea into his masterpiece.

Protect your valuable ideas the same way you'd protect your VCR, by indelibly marking them as yours. Work out all the details in secrecy, present them in written form to those concerned, get the operation going, leak it to the press (if appropriate), *then* spread the word to your larcenous associates. It's hard to steal yesterday's headlines.

The Godfather: His offers you should refuse, since his little ploys are designed to put you in what he considers your rightful place—at the bottom. He'll "accidentally" forget to return your calls, while calling back your male associates promptly. Or he'll treat you as a glorified secretary, no matter how high your real status is, and ask you to take messages for the males in the firm or perform trivial tasks for him. His tone is polite, but clearly bossy, even though you don't work for him.

To halt this belittling treatment, use the scientific system of training with punishments and rewards, just as you would with any other rat. If he fails to return your calls, try telephoning his superior to get the information, explaining that as Godfather has been out of his office so often lately you had no other way to resolve this important matter. Do this once, and all but the most recalcitrant male will hear your message loud and clear; when I tried it, the offending individual sent me a note the next morning promising to return all future calls of mine instantly if I agreed *never* to contact his boss again.

To push the point home, the next time he demands that you take a message or do a favor (assuming that these aren't legitimate parts of your job), try creative incompetence. Put him on hold for several minutes while you allegedly search for writing materials, repeat his words back extremely slowly as you struggle to record his thoughts verbatim, then "lose" or "forget" to transmit the message. You might also disconnect him occasionally during your hunt for a working pen or joke that you hope that the recipient of the message can decipher your handwriting. With your passive resistance, you'll control the interchange and make him conclude that such tactics are more trouble than they're worth.

The Pseudo-Mentor: He challenges your authority by pretending that you have none. After listening to your presentation, he'll inquire casually whether you've run these ideas by your male peers at the firm and if you're quite sure that the plan doesn't need a bit more fine-tuning. He'll also offer you gratuitous advice on how to handle yourself in the business world, point out any minor mistakes of yours with relish and generally present himself as a senior statesman helping out a complete novice.

Cope with him through role reversal. Imply that in your view it's he that lacks the decison-making authority. A good way to do this is through negative selling: Pose series of qualifying questions, such as how many people he'd have to consult before being able to make a ten-thousand-dollar deal for the firm or who he'd have to consult before implementing plans of a certain type, before giving him even an inkling of your idea. Challenge him by suggesting that you'd be happy to present these ideas to his superiors in the interest of expediting a decision, and then let him talk you into dealing with him. Once he's been put on the defensive about his own power, you'll be back in control again.

The Abominable Snowman: Whenever you speak with him, his icy tone gives you the uncomfortable sensation that you've thoroughly alienated him in some mysterious manner. It's plain that he just doesn't like you and is only tolerating your telephone presence out of sheer business necessity. But what's he got against you anyway? You've tried to warm him up with a few friendly remarks, done homework before the call to present yourself professionally and *know* your telephone transactions are genuinely important and appropriately handled. And yet the more you try to reach out to him, the colder the reception you get from him.

If this reminds you of someone on your Rolodex, chances are that you've encountered the hard-core misogynist. It's not that he dislikes you personally—what he hates is the whole feminine sex. However, by working against his stereotypes, you can thaw him out enough to establish a professional relationship. Since he usually believes that all women are inefficient, overly emotional, too sensitive and prone to gossip, counter his stereotypes by announcing the topic of your call the instant you have him on the line and hanging up the second you have his reply—maintaining a brusque, just-the-facts tone throughout. You'll never win his heart, but you can at least win his respect.

ESCAPING THE SECRETARIAL STEREOTYPE

How do you counter sexist putdowns if you're a secretary or administrative assistant? Although many secretaries are using their position to clamber up the corporate ladder or are already performing the tasks of high-level bosses, some callers may still react to you as a potentially incompetent underling or as a handy scapegoat to blame for your employer's elusiveness or failure to return their calls. You may also find yourself the target of sexist or sexually suggestive comments as a result of your sex and position.

Your dilemma is to shatter the stereotypes, while conducting yourself in the courteous, professional manner dictated by your office. A good first step is to introduce yourself to callers by name, which will help personalize you in their minds. Avoid an overfriendly approach; responding to calls with, "Mr. Harrigan's office, Sally speaking," will detract from your professional image and might encourage unwanted intimacies. Instead, give your full name, both when receiving and placing calls for your employer: "This is Barbara Kennedy calling for Eleanor Smith. Is Mr. Brown available to take her call?"

Continue to establish your professional image by learning the caller's name as early as possible and interjecting it into the conversation periodically. Revealing appropriate knowledge will also improve your image; you might say, if true, "Mrs. Brown has been hoping to speak with you today" or "I enjoyed reading your remarks in our trade journal." Demonstrating a general interest, without obtrusive questioning, subtly highlights your professional approach.

Reflect this attitude also by taking responsibility. Don't pass the buck by saying, "That's not my department" or "I don't know"; show a little initiative by offering to determine who can handle the matter and having him or her call back, or summarizing the problem succinctly in a message to your employer. Read back the message to reassure the caller that his words and number will be relayed accurately, commenting, "I'll see that he gets this news as soon as he gets back" or "I'll put this message on her desk immediately." Show him that you care about your work, and he'll treat you with more respect.

As you apply these tactics, let go of the attitude—if you have it—that you are "just a secretary." The suggestion of this sentiment in your voice can encourage the would-be sexist in his misguided approach; and it can turn into a self-fulfilling prophecy for you. Instead share you conviction that you are an important member of the corporate team—which you are. He'll hear that strong, confident self-image in your words and manner and react positively.

SEX AND THE SINGLE TELEPHONE

Flirting on the phone can be fun—with the right person. But if a business caller proves to be one of those receiver Romeos who feels compelled to flirt with any female in listening range, it's an annoyance. The worst offenders, I've found, are salesmen; some of them operate under the illusion that compliments on your lovely voice or suggestive remarks will stimulate your lust to buy. The compulsive phone flirt may also believe that you will be complimented by his unbusinesslike propositions, just as construction workers seem to assume that we enjoy their wolf whistles and lewd remarks about our anatomy.

To block unwelcome phone passes, act assertively at the first hint of familiarity. Silence at the first "sweetheart" or "baby" from him may seem to give consent to move to further intimacies. Give him a polite brush-off by saying something like, "I'd prefer that you called me Susan [or Ms. Jones]. But go on about the KMJ merger . . ." If he then pursues the point, maintaining that he was "just trying to be friendly," or if he accuses you of being "one of those women's libbers," don't be tempted into apologies or explanations of your position. Just repeat your previous statement firmly and steer the conversation back to business.

Compliments about your voice or other personal attributes should also be dealt with politely, but firmly. If the remark is fairly mild, wait a beat or two, then deliver a deflating thanks, but no thanks, like this: "Nice of you. Now I'd like to *voice* a few unlovely objections to the contract you propose." For more ardent or suggestive remarks, a bit of humor can be effective. During a seemingly routine business call, a male editor I knew informed me that he'd love to meet an attractive virgin. Astonished, I replied that I considered myself a *literary* matchmaker only, but perhaps he'd like to meet a nice romance novel I had on my list.

Sometimes it's difficult to judge if a male associate has business affairs or romantic affairs on his mind, as when he suggests meeting for cocktails to discuss some current project. Or perhaps he's proposing some joint venture of an apparently businesslike nature that requires spending a good deal of time together. Is it a subtle come-on or a profitable opportunity? When you're unsure, let the phone be your chaperone, by saying that with your hectic schedule it's hard to get away from the office, so you'll call him next week about it.

Suppose "Hot Lips" decides on the direct approach and phones you for a date? If you're not interested, the problem becomes one of turning him down without turning him off to dealing with you on a business basis in the future. When I was single, I found the best approach was to avoid the "I have a boyfriend" response, since it gives the man a momentary entree into your personal life, and to say, in a faintly wistful but resolute tone, "I'm sorry, but my policy is never to mix business with pleasure."

WOMAN POWER!

While our sex may encounter some obstacles as we establish ourselves professionally, we also enjoy some phone advantages. The trick is knowing how to use femininity *positively*. It's a mistake, I feel, to stoop to deceptive tactics like pretending your cold call is a personal communication by saying to a new prospect's screener, "Tell Bob that Sandy is calling." Using sexiness to manipulate men in business situations damages our image and raises suspicions; maintaining a friendly distance engenders rapport and trust.

What we should do instead is capitalize on our assets, such as the network of potentially supportive female allies we have at all levels of the work world. These bonds of sisterhood help us build rapport with the secretaries who decide whose calls to put through to their employers, let us trade potentially valuable information with women at our own level to the advantage of both parties, and enable us to grow professionally through our contacts with role models and mentors above us on the corporate ladder.

Our feminine traits can also help us establish strong rapport with male associates. Since women are viewed as less threatening than men, it's easier for us to penetrate male defenses and ensure that our message is heard and acted upon in the initial telephone contact with a man. After that crucial first impression, it's your performance, rather than sex, that will register—you as the consummate *professional*.

PART TWO: PROFITS

Practical
Strategies for
Common
Business
Situations

7

SECRETS OF A POWERHOUSE PRESENTATION

Whether you're making cold calls or contacting likely buyers you already know, a powerful presentation can make the difference between a sale and a lost opportunity. That's why ad-libbing your pitch is risky; when you're pulling concepts out of the air, it's easy to overlook the most potentially telling sales point, find yourself ill-prepared to counter obvious objections or actually *unsell* a prospect with off-putting wording or an inadvertently negative message. Investing a few extra minutes in perfecting your pitch will pay off—not by selling everyone you call—but by increasing your odds of turning a "maybe" into a definite "yes."

Here's how to create a message that arouses buying interest:

• **Identify some hot buttons.** Hanging your presentation on an appealing benefit—not feature—of your product or service makes strong psychological sense. Which is more likely to entice you to buy a car: the exact dimensions of its engine, or the powerful and sexy feeling you'll have as you zip along the highway in your new turbo? And what tempts you to order garden supplies: a desire to possess a bag of scientifically developed grass seed, or a mental image of having a lush, green lawn that your neighbors will admire and envy?

Sex and status aren't the only buying triggers. According to psychological theory, our behavior revolves around two motives: to avoid pain and to increase pleasure. Both elements can figure in a pitch: a security system spares its owners the monetary and emotional *pain* of crimes against themselves or their property, and thus affords them the *pleasure* of knowing that they've effectively protected their family or business from danger. Other enticements that might figure into a presentation are the promise of more fun, bigger profits, faster results, better service, lower costs, fewer mistakes and increased convenience.

• **Create the right emotional climate.** Since the prospect may not be in the correct mood to fully appreciate your concept, use your qualifying questions to increase his or her receptivity to it. Often when I'm calling editors to offer a major book, I'll start the conversation by asking, "Bought anything *big* lately?" As they mentally relive some negotiating triumph, a desire to recapture those exciting, powerful feelings is born. Or what they may be recalling is their frustration at losing a big one during a previous auction, and they may be thinking that now's the time to even the score. Either way, they're primed to buy before they even know what I'm selling.

A provocative question or two isn't the only way to grab initial attention. An intriguing statement can also set the stage for your presentation by hinting at the attractions to come. It would be a mistake to announce baldly that you're calling to sell the prospect on a new computer service program, since he might well say no before you can explain the benefits. Instead, you might stir him up a little by saying, "Mr. Prospect, our organization has been working with several companies like yours who were amazed to discover that they were wasting money every day on unnecessary or improper service."

• **Paint vivid mental pictures.** Helping your prospect visualize the product or service in her imagination is a powerful sales tool in telephone selling. It's also a good way to get the customer to reveal the needs and desires that will help you sell her. Let's say you are offering a wide range of home repair services and are cold-calling local homeowners. Rather than open with a shopping list of your services, most of which would not be of interest to that particular prospect, you might enlist her aid by asking her to imagine her home lovingly restored or repaired by a team of highly skilled, European-trained craftsmen.

All of these words evoke positive mental images. By saying "home" instead of "house," you subtly stimulate the emotions we all feel about our place of residence. The phrase "lovingly restored" sounds warm and friendly, while addressing her natural concern about the quality of the workmanship. It encourages her to maintain that mental picture of her home perfected. Your next words, "European-trained craftsmen," reinforces the image of high standards, while adding a touch of glamour and cachet to the idea.

• **Try role reversal.** A common mistake of the inexperienced salesperson is to underestimate the intelligence of the prospect. While it makes sense to avoid twenty-dollar words and fanciful metaphors that might confuse an inattentive listener, too many baby-simple concepts will sound patronizing. Also, if you spell out every idea to the utmost, you miss out on the potential for audience participation. Given a little encouragement, some of your prospects will actually sell themselves.

Instead of making hand-holding statements like, "Temporary office help enables you to handle your peak periods at lower cost," try challenging the prospect to name some ways she'd benefit from the service. You might say, "With your office management experience, you could probably think of several ideas for cost-effective use of temporary help during peak periods." Use any thoughts she does come up with as a sales fulcrum. Or if she fails to take the bait, offer a leading remark or two: "Many of our customers especially welcome the opportunity to reevaluate their employee needs weekly and arrange to have enough personnel on hand to provide the kind of service their customers expect."

DRAMATIZING THE FACTS

The most potent pitches first appeal to the prospect's emotions, arousing an urgent, primal impulse to *buy right now,* then address the needs of his superego with reasonable and logical justifications for that decision. However, you don't want the main body of your product story to seem anticlimactic or filled with boring technical details. What you want instead is an accurate product description that presents the vital statistics in a catchy, exciting manner.

To structure the factual element of your presentation, write down the key features of the product and arrange them in order of importance. Let's imagine that your computer software package is designed to prevent and repair hard disk errors. You might start off your presentation with a brief but alarming description of the hard disk disasters that a computer user like your prospect might encounter: perhaps having the disk just quit operation in the midst of preparing the employee payroll or customer billings.

Now that the customer is vividly imagining himself the

victim of some mysterious computer malfunction that costs him time and money, you'd point out benefit number one— that the product can actually recover data losses *after* they happen. After explaining how this is accomplished, you'd then move to the second benefit—that the product automatically reviews every single byte and bit on the hard disk for errors every day and corrects the problems *before* you even know that they exist. You could then follow up by pointing out that the daily check-up takes just five minutes, and requires no operator input as it is fully automatic.

As you develop your script, aim at a natural, conversational style, rather than the stiff, formal English that was drilled into most of us in school. Don't hesitate to include colloquial expressions or break a few rules of grammar. Ending a sentence with a preposition, or splitting a few infinitives, can give your words the ring of spontaneity, while a starchy style may sound "canned" and unnatural. Also you don't want to make the prospect uncomfortable with his or her poor speech habits through hypercorrectness.

MAGIC WORDS

Twelve words that have an extraordinary power to persuade, according to a study by the Department of Psychology at Yale University, are:

- you
- new
- proven
- love
- money
- easy
- results
- free
- save
- discovery
- help
- guarantee

Mark Twain once wrote that the difference between the right word and the almost right word is the difference between lightning and the lightning bug. Here's a look at how you can increase the impact of your message with a little rewriting:

So-so word	Power word
• up-to-date	• state-of-the-art
• good	• outstanding
• useful	• invaluable
• quiet	• soundless, whisper-soft
• interesting	• intriguing, fascinating, captivating
• unusual	• innovative, radical, unique
• skill	• expertise, brilliance, genius
• price	• investment
• better	• superior
• increase	• double, multiply
• improve	• enrich, ex-pand
• problem	• challenge, hurtle
• high	• skyrocket-ing
• deal	• opportunity
• would	• will
• could, would	• can, will
• important	• urgent, vital

PREEMPTING POTENTIAL OBJECTIONS

Do many of your prospects raise the same objection, or do you anticipate resistance on one of your points? A good way to defuse such sales obstacles is to build a winning reply right into your basic pitch. Naturally, you'll want to express the message in positive terms, thus avoiding a defensive tone that will work against you.

It's also wise to prepare solid rebuttal arguments for any objections you hear fairly frequently. These shouldn't be part of the actual presentation but held in reserve as additional sales ammunition to be deployed when necessary. Anticipating every conceivable criticism of your concept and addressing it in your pitch could actually plant negative ideas in the prospect's mind—exactly what you wish to avoid. Instead, your approach should be modelled after the somewhat dour New England proverb "Hope for the best, but prepare for the worst."

If you look at typical sales objections carefully, you'll see that the worst is often not so bad. While it's natural to be disheartened by any implied or direct criticism of your product or service, a negative comment could actually represent a disguised sales opportunity. By fluently countering the objection, you'll have leapt over one of the hurdles lying between you and the sale, and that bit of forward momentum may be enough to close the deal.

DEFEATING THE DEADLY SEVEN

Here's a list of seven not-so-deadly objections, and how to turn them around:

• **"I can't afford it."** True or false? As a salesperson you must take the optimistic stance in addressing this common excuse not to buy. One line of attack is the "pennies a day" approach, in which you reduce the cost down to a manageable level. It's hard for the prospect to argue that he can't afford, say, seven cents a day for the exciting, vital product you're offering. Or you might use clever calculations to show how he'd really *save* substantial sums—or increase his income—by investing in the product.

Another good tactic is judicious flattery. Your line might be something like: "I appreciate your concern about cost, but

I've found that an important person like yourself usually has some money tucked away for the right opportunity." Then you'd go on explaining why this extraordinary value is indeed that chance he's been waiting for, by describing some additional benefits of the product.

• **"It costs too much."** This can be handled with the pennies-per-day explanation or arguments focusing on the high quality of the product. You might argue that while price is a one-time expense, bargain products can have the annoying habit of costing time and money over and over, generally at the most inconvenient moments. Then you could describe the superior workmanship and little extras that make your product the better overall buy. If you have a financing plan, you might then explain how the prospect can enjoy these attractive features now, while paying later.

The reason the prospect gives for *not* buying can also be presented as the reason to buy. You might point out that items like life insurance, a new roof or an office security system always "cost too much" until they are actually needed. That's what makes the investment so attractive—the ruinous cost of *not* making it. You might then give some examples culled from local news reports or the experience of other reluctant prospects.

• **"I have a friend/relative in the business."** Lee Iacocca, the head of Chrysler Motors, seems to have identified the psychological reality that will help you overcome this objection: "When money talks, ideology walks." Most of your prospects are sufficiently pragmatic to put the bottom line ahead of mere affection. In taking this approach, subtlety is vital, since you're proposing a form of treason. What you might say is, "Our company places a high value on loyalty. However, I'm sure you'd agree that there are many sources of profitable opportunities. For example, right now we're in touch with some special situations that . . ."

A related approach, should the special opportunity tactic fail to take hold, is the compromise close. You might suggest that you don't want to take business away from that valued friend but are instead proposing that your ideas will actually expand the size of the pie. The friend can have his accustomed share, while your aim is to get the *extra* business that your concepts will generate. If your reasoning works, the prospect may then agree to let you have at least part of his trade.

Knocking the competition, on the other hand, can create the "Romeo and Juliet effect," where the prospect rebels against your disapproval by embracing his present supplier even more tightly. Even if your opinion is sought, the best line is that the other firm is a fine one but not currently offering the opportunity that you're describing (if true, of course).

• **I want to think it over/discuss it with X"** or *"I'm not in the market right now."* If you're suspecting that these are stalls, you're probably right. Many prospects hate to say harsh words like, "No," and prefer instead to postpone the reckoning to the indefinite future. Your tactic should be to create urgency by stressing the importance of timing. Perhaps the particular price you offer is available for a limited time, or a price increase is likely in the future (usually true in these inflationary times); the product will sell out due to the strong demand you've already encountered; or other buyers are already competing for this unique item.

Another point that can be made effectively is that by deciding immediately, the prospect can start enjoying the benefits (you may wish to review one or two of your most compelling arguments here) *right now*. So why deprive oneself of this pleasure, especially since it costs as little or less to do so right away as it will in the future? You might also observe that in your experience, it's not how long you think about something that's important, but that it's making the *right* decision. Add that you'd be glad to help him think about it, by supplying additional information.

- **"Send me some literature."** Another stalling tactic, or way to refuse without actually saying, "No." Move forward with remarks like, "I'd be glad to, but there are some aspects that are best explained 'live.' For example . . ." Another tactic is to use the request as a launching pad for your qualifying procedures, as in "I will, but let's explore for a moment which aspects you'd like to learn more about. Do you use . . .?"

- **"It isn't as good as what we're using now."** Competition is a fact of business life, and your rebuttals have to address the problem of brand loyalty effectively. Here's where a bit of research comes in handy; with an in-depth knowledge of your competitors' strengths and weaknesses, you construct persuasive replies to the question of "Why should I give you my business when we've done so well with company X?" Imagine the effect of replying, "Because their mutual fund pays a 7.5 percent return, while ours *doubles* your money in just eight years."

What if you're waging a David versus Goalith battle against a competitor whose size and track record make it an acknowledged industry leader, or which has carved out a best-seller niche for its main product? These strengths can be turned around to create a winning position for your firm: Perhaps you deliver the sort of personal service conspicuously absent in the vast bureaucracy of your rival. Or you could present your firm as an ambitious comer destined to be the next IBM—but currently offering an outstanding bargain to the savvy few.

• **"I don't need/want it."** While this may well be true, a little diplomatic probing does sometimes pay off. If you are calling an established customer, it's a good opportunity to educate yourself as to the needs and interests of the firm. You might say, "Okay, but may I ask why?" Your prospect will often be sufficiently relieved at being let off the hook so easily that he'll reveal his true objection. If you perceive that a misunderstanding about the product or service is the barrier, you can move to a softer sell, ready to retreat if the customer's resistance seems to stiffen.

On the other hand, in a cold call, you might as well go for a harder sell, with a rejoinder like: "Other people have told me the same thing *before they tried it*. After they did, I've often been told that . . ." Then illustrate the point with some vivid success stories. A good rule of thumb in deciding when additional selling will be counterproductive is to give up after you've been turned down three times or after a refusal so emphatically firm that you are virtually certain that the prospect's next move will be to hang up on you.

CLOSING IN ON THE PROSPECT

How do you know exactly when your words have heated up enough interest to produce an order? Take your customer's temperature periodically with a trial close. If the customer is ready to buy, further talk is not only a waste of time but could actually cost you the sale should one of your additional points misfire. If your presentation is planned correctly, in most cases you should have delivered enough information in the first three minutes to make your first request for an order (or appointment, if that's the goal of the call).

A good way of applying a little buying pressure is to take a point the customer has responded favorably to—or an objection you've successfully overcome—and use it as your bridge to the order request. You might say, "Since you agree that car leasing makes good tax sense for your organization, why don't we discuss which makes and models you'd prefer?" If a new objection is unearthed at this point, you can return smoothly to the pitch; if not, you've advanced several additional steps down the road to commitment.

Here are some other closing tactics to try:

• **Use positive choices to close.** Make it difficult to say no by posing questions that don't permit a negative answer, such as: "Do you prefer red or black?" or "Shall I send it by parcel post or private courier service?" The idea is to avoid confronting the buyer with a major decision—whether or not to order—by posing instead a series of minor, easy-to-make choices. As you offer option after option, the order is completed without your ever having to make a point-blank request for it.

• **Let agreement become a habit.** Another method to lead the prospect step-by-step to a commitment through questions is to lard your whole pitch with leading questions that are almost certain to get a "yes" response. Each of these "yeses" represents a tiny mental commitment to the concept and increases the prospect's feeling of rapport with you, making it that much harder for the prospect to suddenly reverse himself when the most important question of all is posed: "Shall I write up your order now?"

• **Assuming the sale.** Rather than ask for the sale or close in with questions, another tactic is to make positive statements that *assume* that the order's already been made: "Since you're sending out over three hundred packages a week, I'm putting you down for our 4000 model postage meter, that will give you the speed and flexibility you need." Statements like this can be combined with presumptive questions like: "Would you also like a mailing cart to go with it? It's a hundred dollars extra."

• **Suggest a package deal.** Once you've had a chance to size up the prospect, make ordering easy by proposing a specific group of purchases or an order of a particular size: "I've found that new parents like yourself usually find that they need their child's portrait in a variety of sizes, so that all the relatives can get one. That why I recommend our 'G' package with thirty-two wallet-sized, eight three-by-fives, six five-by-sevens, and four eight-by-tens. You'll save over twenty dollars over the cost of individual orders and have the pictures right now, when you need them."

• **Make it a challenge to close.** Although the usual sales advice is to be friendly, agreeable and supportive of the prospect, some reluctant prospects respond better to a touch of negativity, I've found. Recently I had a telephone discussion with an editor about a magazine article I wanted to write. My enthusiastic description seemed to interest him, but he was vague about committing himself to a contract and firm price. Switching to the negative sell, I said, "Before we go on, are you *sure* you can meet my price of a dollar a word?" A minute or so later, he not only offered full price but threw in a generous expense account.

• **Close with openness.** There's also something to be said for skipping the subtleties and psychological ploys and just asking for the order—again and again, if necessary. Some of the most successful salespeople I know rely on a "nothing up my sleeves" approach. With refreshing candor, they break the traditional taboos and use four letter words like "sell" in their pitches. Their attitude is: "I *know* that you're going to buy, and pretty soon you're going to know it too." And, more often than not, they're absolutely right!

8

MAKING PROFITABLE CONNECTIONS

I once spent three minutes on the phone and hung up twenty thousand dollars richer. That's what I call dialing for dollars—I made about $110 for each *second* I was on the line. Lift up your receiver, and you could be seconds away from an equally profitable sale—or an even bigger one. Business case history after case history proves that the shortest distance between two points—the customer's checkbook and your bank account—is a telephone line. That's because phone selling multiplies sales opportunities: In a single day, you could contact as many as one hundred prospects, while the salesperson in the field averages just eight sales visits.

Phone sales are also the cheapest way to deliver your sales story. Dictate a letter to a prospect—which he or she may not read or act upon—and you may spend ten dollars; visit him at his office and you might spend as much as one hundred in time and travel expenses only to discover he's not interested or out; but dial his number, and for mere pennies you can sell him with a personalized pitch, address his objections and close the deal. And the bargain is likely to get even better in the future; studies show that phone costs have historically risen far more slowly than the overall consumer price index.

Not only does phone selling cut costs, but it also expands your sales territory, allowing you to capture customers outside of your immediate geographical area. With an appropriate product or service, your marketplace can be an entire nation—or you could even develop an international clientele. There are, after all, more than one billion phones in the world, putting profitable connections with potential customers anywhere in today's global village as close as your fingertips—and your imagination.

PROFITABLE PROSPECTING

An entrepreneur I know told me that the secret of her success is that she considers prospecting a twenty-four-hour-a-day priority. Each time she picks up the receiver—whether it's to receive an order, to answer a customer inquiry, or merely to chat with a friend—she routinely asks for the names of others who might be interested in her product. The "hot list" of names she's gathered by spending a few extra seconds on each call have enabled her to nearly triple her volume of business.

A local real estate agent gained a competitive advantage by telephoning property owners in prime neighborhoods *before they entered the marketplace*. Her secret weapon for these targeted cold calls was one of the over two-hundred "crisscross" or "reverse" phone books, titled *City Cross-Reference Directory*, published by Cole Publications (901 West Bond Street, Lincoln, NE 68521, phone 405-473-9715). Covering most of the U.S. and parts of Canada, these books are published annually, cost between one hundred and five hundred dollars, depending on the geographic area covered and include sections that: (1) list all phone subscribers by street address, (2) list names of subscribers according to phone number, (3) give the names, titles and occupations of tenants in local office buildings, (4) list the names and numbers of newcomers to the area, (5) rate the income and buying power of residents by street, (6) include census tract maps of the entire area with wealth ratings, (7) do the same by zip code and (8) provide detailed demographics that allow you to select trade areas by such factors as percentage with children under age twelve or median years of schooling.

Other helpful directories that may be available at your library include:

• **Thomas Register of American Manufacturers.** An annual multivolume directory which lists manufacturers alphabetically by product, including addresses and branch offices, phone numbers, executive's names, capital rating. Company catalogs are also included.

• **Million Dollar Directory.** A multivolume directory with details on the 120,000 largest companies in the U.S., organized alphabetically, geographically and by SIC (Standard Industrial Classification) product code.

• **Encyclopedia of Associations.** Supplemented quarterly, this publication lists thousands of organized groups in the U.S. with names and addresses, descriptions of activities and publications and dates of conventions and meetings. There's also a separate "Geographic and Executive Index."

• **Standard and Poor's Register of Corporations, Directors and Executives.** A three-volume listing of thirty-seven-thousand corporations with key personnel, with alphabetical entries both by company name and by the names of executives and directors. Also classifies the firms geographically and by product code.

Your librarian can also help you find the key directories for your specific field. In my profession, publishing, I frequently consult *Literary Market Place* (for contacts at book publishers), *Magazine Market Place* and *Writer's Market* (for detailed marketing information for both book and magazine publishers).

Another source of information that you can profit from is the "people" section of your trade journal. Associates who have just switched companies or been promoted to higher positions at their current firm are usually eager to start doing business—and this could be an opportunity to strengthen an existing relationship or cultivate a new buyer. With a simple congratulatory call—and a few words of soft sell for your products or services—you could generate both goodwill and buying interest. Or if an in-person presentation strikes you as more desirable, now's also the time to suggest a get-together, before his or her calendar gets full.

A personnel recruiter finds that prospects are delivered to his door daily, in the local paper. What he does is look for news about corporate relocations to his area—then he calls the firm to offer his services in locating qualified employees from the area. Alternatively, if a company is moving *out* of his area, he'll contact desirable employees from the firm who may be unhappy about the move, and dangle enticing local job opportunities in front of them.

You can also capitalize on unpublicized changes—if you position yourself to exploit them. Taking a friendly interest in the activities of your established customers, currently inactive accounts and any likely prospects can help you uncover hidden sales opportunities. Your call at the right psychological moment may be just the nudge that's needed to turn yesterday's reluctant prospect into today's new customer, resuscitate a marginal or inactive account or increase the ordering volume of one of your existing customers.

Timing your calls according to the likely buying cycles of

your prospects and customers is another excellent way to generate sales. With a little industry research, your selling overtures could soon be directed at those who are already in a receptive, buying mood. A simple "Hello" call may be all it takes to get an order, while a failure to keep in touch could cause good customers to be seduced away by your more energetic competitors.

Sometimes it pays to remind your prospects of your existance even if you have no special reason to think they want to buy right then. During a routine conversation with an editor, I had the happy inspiration to ask about her "wish list," the books she'd like to acquire. What she urgently wanted, she said, was a book on marketing magazine articles with query letters. Although she was the editor of a book I'd already written on making magazine article sales, clearly my name had not entered her mind for the project. I proposed myself and made the sale in seconds.

FINDING COMMITMENT-MINDED CUSTOMERS

A successful media consultant once told me that she'd signed up with a videodating service so that she'd meet men who were "qualified buyers," those who were ready, able and willing to make a romantic commitment. Courting potential customers effectively also dictates that you identify prospects who are genuinely in the marketplace and avoid time-consuming flirtations with those who lack the power to consummate a sale.

But how do you find that corporate Mr. or Ms. Right? Finding the correct link on the chain of command at medium- or large-sized companies is one of the key challenges of telephone sales. You'll want to avoid being shuttled back and forth between departments in endless search of a decision-maker, or being intercepted along the way by a lower-level employee who turns you down. What you want to do instead is pinpoint your ultimate contact as early on as you can and focus your efforts on getting the ear of that individual.

Where many callers go astray is in asking the wrong person for directions. Recognizing that the object of their quest is likely to lie somewhere in the middle of the organization, they identify the correct department—say, advertising and promotion—and ask to be put in touch with it. Their next move is to query the person who picks up the line in the desired division as to who holds the correct degree of authority. The error of this approach is that you may well be asking the person who is guarding the gate for the key to access—hardly the most effective tactic in presenting an image of authority and competence.

You'll do better by starting at the bottom and recruiting the company receptionist or switchboard operator as your "deep throat." These employees see their role as *helping* callers to gain access to the correct party, rather than intercepting them through screening. Your dialog might go like this:

You: Who's the manager of your advertising and promotion department?
Operator: That would be Dawn Raymond. Shall I connect you?
You: Who does Ms. Raymond report to?
Operator: Michael Pittsfield, our advertising director.
You: And who would be his superior?
Operator: I believe that's Angela Babson.
You: What's her title?
Operator: Vice-president of marketing.
You: Please connect me with Ms. Babson.

If the switchboard operator isn't as forthcoming as you'd like or tries to refer you to a junior employee or the personnel department, a second approach is to start the search at the top, with a request to be connected to the president's office. If the top person's the informal sort, you may find that you have just gained an audience with the ultimate buyer in the firm. Even if he or she doesn't bite personally, this executive is likely to designate someone else of importance as being more receptive to your pitch. Exploit your referral from the boss to gain rapid interest from the specified individual: "I was just on the line with Jackson Potters, who suggested that I contact you."

Similarly, if you succeed only in getting the top executive's assistant, you're almost certain to find him or her a knowledgeable guide to the organizational maze. The secretary's referral and name could also be the wedge you need: "I was just speaking with Michael Potters' secretary, who suggested that I contact you about this matter."

Once you have the magic name, don't be too dazzled to probe a bit with some qualifying questions. It's human nature to inflate one's importance and authority; so counter this tendency tactfully with such questions as, "Are you in a position to make a decision about X today?" or "Would you like me to set up a conference call with you and the others at your organization who'd be involved in this type of decision?" That way you'll escape the frustration of having delivered your whole song and dance only to hear, "I'll have to give this information to my associates and get back to you."

PENETRATING THEIR DEFENSES

Once you've gotten a line on some promising prospects, how do you get *them* on the line to hear your pitch? Although some high ranking executives and business owners do answer their own phones, most of your calls will be fielded by secretaries, administrative assistants or other screeners. By expecting— and preparing for—these encounters you'll acquire the confident, businesslike tone that gets you through to important decision-makers quickly.

Since the degree of screening you'll encounter can vary

from a token inquiry about your name to a rigorous cross-examination, you will need a range of calling strategies. Here are some tactics to keep in mind:

• **Start with a direct request.** Although most of your calls to prospects at large or medium-sized firms will be screened, it's possible you're phoning one of the exceptions or have called in the temporary absence of the screener. In either case, you may be just three words away from immediate access to your party. Here's the formula: "Virginia Smith, please."

What's particularly effective about this wording is that it is *not* a question, but a courteous command. If you'd phrased it as, "Is Virginia Smith in?" however, you'd have introduced a subtle note of suspicion in the greeter's mind. It makes it plain that your call is not anticipated by Ms. Smith—otherwise you'd know she was in—and therefore it may be an unwelcome one. Perhaps, the greeter reasons to her- or himself, some screening is indicated after all.

• **Present yourself with authority.** Suppose your request to be connected is parried by a request for your name. How you announce yourself can spell the difference between the intended recipient of your call being told by his secretary, "Mr. X is on the phone. It sounds important" and "Sounds like some salesman. Shall I get rid of him for you?" Making the right impression on the screener with an effective introduction keeps you from hitting a dead end in your initial effort to reach buying authority.

Often the best reply is just to announce your name and put the ball back in the assistant's court with a question of your own: "It's Lisa Collier Cool. Is she in, please?" Then you'll be in a position to evaluate whether to allow further screening or to place your call at a more opportune moment.

If polite insistence persuades the screener to announce

you at this point, I've discovered that the other person will often take the call out of mere curiosity, even is he or she has never heard your name before. Or she may assume, mistakenly, that she has had previous contact with you—few of us consider our memories completely infallible.

• **Give away your secrets sparingly.** Volunteering information can work against you. When you answer questions you haven't been asked—such as giving the nature of your business when only your name has been requested—each unsolicited nugget of information increases the odds of the screener deciding to probe further, or worse still to tackle the handling of your call herself. One assistant I know who normally screens lightly has been amazed by some callers' compulsion to confess all. Not surprisingly, these are the people she's *most* apt to deny access to her boss.

Whether or not you should reveal the name of your firm along with your own is a trickier question. If others in your firm have already established a business relationship with the prospect, or you're confident that the name will be a door-opener for other reasons, then use it to help sell the other person on speaking with you. If it's unfamiliar or possibly off-putting (perhaps by making your sales objective overly obvious), preserving your aura of mystery is the wiser strategy.

If you've elected to withhold your company affiliation, and the screener follows up with a request for it, complete your reply by again asking to be connected: "I'm with the ABC company. Would you tell Ms. Smith that I'm on the phone, please." You've asked three times now to be connected, while demonstrating that you've nothing to hide. What the screener is hearing is that you judge your call to be important and expect it to be taken by the other person. Frequently this is enough to end the screening. Your odds of success are enhanced by the right tone—avoid sounding defensive or confrontational.

• **Package your calling purpose attractively.** If you encounter a more rigorous screener, the next question is likely to be either "What is the nature of your call?" or "Will Mr. X know what this is in reference to?" What you need here is an answer that will justify the screener's decision to announce you and arouse the interest or curiosity of the intended recipient.

A successful stockbroker who makes cold calls to top-level executives has mastered the delicate balance between candor and come-on in dealing with such questions. To avoid being classed as another stock jockey or hearing the secretary dismiss him with, "Mr. Brown already has a broker," he creates urgency by saying: "I'm calling from New York about an important financial matter at the suggestion of Ms. X, a senior partner here at XYZ Investment Bank." Executives often interpret this as a prelude to a tender offer for the firm—and pick up the line immediately.

His second step, once the prospect is on the line, is to say immediately, "Mr. Brown, I'm not calling to sell you anything. At XYZ Investment Bank, we've been in touch with some *special situations*, and I'd like to know if I come up with something interesting in the next two weeks, would you like to hear about it?" The prospect is immediately disabused of the idea that he's been tricked into getting on the phone.

If your objective is to make an appointment so that you can give your sales presentation face-to-face, another tactic to try is to ask early in the screening process whether or not the delegate handles the boss's calendar. Even if the answer is no— as it usually is—by directing the discussion to a suitable date, you divert attention away from the subject of your call. If it's yes, on the other hand, you may be able to set a date even before you speak with the prospect.

• **Don't sell to secretaries.** Including the word "sell" to your statement of purpose is fatal. Either you'll waste time pitching to an intermediary, who is only empowered to say no; or you'll hit stalling tactics like: "Mr. Franklin is extremely busy right now/about to go on vacation/tied up in meetings all week." Instead, consider wording your objective to include a key benefit of the product or service: "I'm calling about a plan to eliminate phone company overcharges from his bill and secure a refund for those that have occurred within the past five years."

The higher the resistance you anticipate, the vaguer your phrasing should be. Without being deceptive, many sales pitches could reasonably be described as being about "an important business matter," "a plan for company expansion," "a letter I wrote him" or "to set up an appointment." To reduce the odds of having a description like this dissected further, you might follow with, "It will only take a moment, and I know he'll want to hear about this right away."

What if you're asked directly if you are selling something? Rather than try to outsmart the screener with some tricky reply, or sound as if you're confessing some shameful secret, why not take her into your confidence in an appealing way with something like this: "Since Ms. X and our organization are both very active in the telecommunications area, I'm calling to introduce myself and discuss a business proposal about time-sharing. It'll only take a moment or two."

Suppose, despite your best efforts, the secretary divines that you are indeed selling something and turns you down or instructs you to send literature. Rather than slink off the line in defeat, why not give it one last try with words like these: "I understand that you want to protect Ms. Big from unimportant calls. But this will interest her because . . ." Then give a strong sales message listing a key benefit of the product or service, followed by your firm request to hear Ms. Big's opinion directly from her own lips.

• **Address the screener as a fellow professional.** Since the impression you make on the secretary or screener can be crucial to whether or not you get through, make sure to present yourself in a businesslike manner. The secretaries I've interviewed complain of callers treating them as obstacles to get past or dismissing them as nonpersons, hopelessly ignorant of company business. Even more irritating, they report, is the salesperson who tries to win them over with transparent flattery or resorts to flirtatious remarks. What these callers fail to realize is that making a bad impression on the screener can easily result in their being announced to his or her superior in a negative manner.

Handle the screener properly, however, and you'll start making a winning impression on those you call before they even lift their receiver to speak with you for the first time. Begin establishing rapport by determining the identity and status of the greeter. At the onset of the conversation, listen carefully to his or her name and use it from time to time during the conversation.

If you are greeted by an unidentified female, don't assume automatically that her gender connotes secretarial status. Politely inquiring, "Am I speaking with Mr. X's assistant?" keeps you from offending any of your contact's female colleagues who may be pinch-hitting at his phone in the temporary absence of the usual delegate.

• **Consider timing the call to bypass the screener.** To avoid losing time to screening, or to increase the odds of reaching an elusive prospect, try calling before nine, after five and during lunchtime—the times when his or her screening defenses are most likely to be absent.

Another good tactic, in larger organizations with PBX service, is to ask the receptionist for your contact's direct dial number. A surprising number of executives do answer their own direct dial calls but never think to keep the number confidential. Not only will you bypass the switchboard, saving time, but you can call before or after orthodox business hours and reach the other person when he's in and less distracted by other business.

HITTING MOVING TARGETS

What if the problem isn't the screener, but the prospect? He or she's invariably not in yet, in a meeting, away from the desk, at lunch, on the other line, left early, at a convention, working at home, out sick, on vacation, not answering the page, elsewhere in the building or just plain out. Here's a look at how you can handle this calling scenario:

Call #1: prospect's out. Since you are currently unknown to the other person, he or she is unlikely to feel much urgency about returning the call. By leaving a message that's not acted upon, you lose face with the person you're trying to reach and weaken your position if you resort to a second call. The screener is now likely to say something along the lines of, "Don't call us, we'll call you," eliminating further calling opportunities.

Instead, use this as an opportunity to entice the screener to share the secrets of the boss's schedule with you. As soon as you are asked to leave a message, convey the impression that you too are a busy, important person of equal status as the screener's superior, by saying, "Sharon, Mr. Madison and I both seem to have hectic schedules, so I'll call back tomorrow. Would you suggest 10 o'clock or three o'clock?" Not only will you gain helpful clues as to the most opportune moment for your call, but you've in effect made an appointment to call—reducing the odds of being rescreened. By using the screener's name, you also imply that you are holding him or her personally responsible for fulfilling the implied promise of connecting you at the specified time.

Call #2. When you reach the screener, you can now capitalize on the relationship you've established in the first call. You might say, "Sharon, it's Wanda DelRey. This morning you indicated that Mr. Madison would be available at two o'clock. Can you connect me now?" If he's still out, your tactics from the first call can be repeated to establish the prime calling hours for the next day or later in the week.

Here it's important to avoid the pitfall of simply asking when the prospect might be available. You risk creating the impression that you have nothing else to do than sit around at the prospect's leisure, waiting to place your call. Also, the screener might be tempted to brush you off with, "Actually, he's very busy all the time, so perhaps it would be better to write him a letter."

Call #3. If you're beginning to suspect that you are dealing with a particularly hard-to-reach individual, now's the time to consider a little escalation. If you have an assistant of your own, try having him or her place the call, announcing that you've previously arranged to contact the prospect at this hour. The image of importance you've already created will be reinforced by an articulate ambassador, and annoying questions about the nature of your business will be deflected.

By building a groundwork of rapport in the two earlier calls, you'll also be in a good position if you must place the call for yourself. Since you've treated the screener with respect while simultaneously establishing your authority, and you've made a point of using her name, chances are that by now she'll *want* you to get through. Her job, after all, is to *assist* those in authority; thus, by positioning yourself correctly, you'll inspire her to throw her knowledge and influence behind your desired goal.

Call #4. Still no luck? While some telephone sellers don't believe in leaving messages because they so seldom get callbacks when they do, others are masterful at baiting the hook with a few provocative words and landing the hard-to-get prospect on their line.

One successful salesman imbues his messages with an air of urgency by including an implied deadline for response. Instead of merely saying, "Ask him to call me when he gets a chance," he'll say firmly, "We would appreciate hearing from him by twelve-thirty." If the screener then objects that the prospect will be unable to comply, the salesman increases his clout by letting *her* negotiate with him until a mutually convenient hour is settled upon.

A mysterious message can also be effective, especially if you anticipate strong sales resistance from the screener or prospect. Executive recruiter Nick Mancino prefers to limit his message to his name and number, reasoning that simple curiosity will often get the prospect to return the call. If pressed by the screener for the nature of his business with her superior, his response is a cryptic, "He'll know." He then departs from the line without revealing another word.

Mancino reports that he's seldom challenged to defend this innocent ploy when his call is returned. If he is, however, he explains that his organization believes in handling personnel searches in a discreet, confidential manner. He then smoothly directs the discussion to possible fits between the prospect's current hiring needs and the candidates he's now placing.

Call #5. If you're tempted to abandon the sales effort after a few unsuccessful calls, consider this cautionary tale a subsidiary rights director of a major publisher told me recently. When it became apparent that her company was about to publish a potential best-seller, she telephoned her usual list of top paying magazines to offer them excerpts. All asked to participate in the auction—except the editor from the best-paying publication of all, who failed to return her calls.

The auction was held, and the rights went for $150,000. A few weeks later, however, she was called by the elusive editor, who demanded to know why he wasn't invited to bid. "It was perfect for us," he complained. "We'd have gone up to four hundred thousand—maybe more." She ruefully recounted her four attempts to reach him. His reply: "Do you have any idea how many people call me every day with a book to peddle? When you've got something *really* hot it's up to you to let us know about it."

But how? The answer, she decided, would have been a really high voltage message like; "Tell him he's got a two-hour exclusive on rights to the hottest book on our next list, the subject of which is so confidential that I can only tell him *personally*." While shock tactics like these should be reserved as a last resort and only used when you *do* have the right stuff to back your audacious approach, persistence and imagination could pay off—sometimes quite handsomely.

9

SELLING YOURSELF

To succeed on the telephone, every call you make should have an underlying sales message: the idea that you are attractive to deal with, thoroughly professional and highly knowledgeable about your business. Convey these messages effectively, and you'll make the ultimate sale—of *yourself*. Once others have bought the idea of you as a welcome, desirable contact to have, making the *second* sale—of your current calling objective—is greatly simplified.

Consider the case of a business acquaintance of mine who has been buying for twenty years from the same salesman, despite the frequent overtures of rival salespeople. Why? According to the buyer: "It's not because his prices are lower— they're about the same as everyone else's. It's not because his product is all that much better than the others'—it isn't. His only secret is that he gives my ego a bit of a massage and makes me feel that he really cares."

Establishing the strong rapport that inspires such loyalty from your customers and other phone contacts is a matter of *consistent* cultivation—starting with your initial telephone conversation with that person and continuing throughout your business relationship. Here's an examination of how to present yourself to win the hearts and accounts of those you call.

THE EXPERTISE FACTOR

To really attack the phone with confidence, you must convince yourself that the other person would not only welcome the chance to speak with you but that she could *profit* from doing so. Along with your wit and charm, you're offering her a real opportunity: it may be the knowledge of how she could cut costs, increase efficiency, acquire vital intelligence, gain clout, solve annoying problems, upgrade professional skills or score some other business coup.

How do you convince the recipients of your calls that you're making an offer they can't refuse? By providing them with the services of an expert—you. Promoting yourself as an insider who can initiate your prospects into the mysteries of your firm and its goods or services encourages prospects to see you as a valued ally in their decision-making.

Acquiring this edge takes only a modest investment of your time. While studying your product's brochures, manuals and ads is a sound strategy, true expertise will require more sophisticated intelligence-gathering. Glean intimate financial details on your company and its competitors from their quarterly or annual reports (available to the public if the company issues stock publicly) and their 10-K filings with the Securities and Exchange Commission (available from the SEC or your stockbroker).

While the best information is gained from frequent networking with others in the industry, keeping up with published news is also important. Your associates are flattered when you refer to coverage they've received in trade journals and the business pages of the local paper; while ignorance of publicly announced changes in their personnel or corporate direction could undermine even the smoothest presentation.

Even if your immediate purpose isn't to make a sale, by cultivating a reputation as an informed source of hot gossip, job leads and the latest industry trends you'll become a more powerful player in almost any calling situation. Your tidbits of information can be traded for present or future favors, exchanged for news you could turn to immediate profit, serve as attention-getting openers with new contacts or be used to enrich existing relationships.

A few years ago, my literary agency happened to accumulate a large number of romance novels to sell. After memorizing the sales figures of the field's best-sellers and acquainting myself with its buzz words (such as "bodice-ripper" for historical saga), I sprinkled each sales pitch with intriguing facts. Normally elusive editors began to call me to ask where the market was heading—and to offer big-money, multibook contracts to the clients I pushed.

BE TERRIFYINGLY RELIABLE

There's power in information. A businessman I know is so meticulously systematic in his work routines that his secretary jokes that he folds his trash precisely in thirds, stamps it with the date and enters a notation in his Filofax before tossing it out. She's exaggerating, but only *slightly*. His meticulous files rival those of the CIA: He's chronicled every business transaction he's made, organized a "tickler file" to keep pending projects on track and maintains intimately detailed files on each player he deals with regularly.

With this secret arsenal of industry intelligence, coupled with a highly developed memory for salient details, he's able to capture—and hold—the initiative in his telephone conversations. He'll often start the call by vividly reminding the other person of their last contact—which is especially impressive if it was, say, an awards ceremony held five years previously. Right away, the prospect is flattered to have been found so memorable, while feeling obscurely guilty about her own weak recall of the event. Now that the correct psychological climate has been established, the prospect will almost inevitably agree to look over whatever project my associate was calling to offer.

Exactly thirty days later, the businessman moves to phase two of the attack. Calling at the earliest possible hour, he again catches the customer with her defenses down and inquires about the status of the project. If, as is often the case, the other person confesses that she's yet to study the materials, he lets her off the hook by offering to call back in ten days. Then he pleasantly inquires about some interesting corporate development at her firm which has *not* been generally announced or congratulates her on her daughter's upcoming nuptials—announced only that morning in the daily paper. She finds herself promising to take prompt action.

On the tenth day, he calls even earlier than usual, which frequently results in the prospect's arriving at work to see his message already on her desk. Embarrassed by her inertia, she's busy skimming over the prospectus—which reads very well—when the businessman calls back, apologizing for having called before her customary hours. Often, this barrage of terrifying efficiency—and her sense of embarrassment at failing to measure up to my associate's expectations—will inspire her to make an offer.

An excellent memory—or excellent organization—can also be your secret weapon. What others—even those endowed with neither of these assets—instinctively recognize is that all of us can remember the things and people we care about. No one needs to remind us to collect our lottery winnings or to arrive promptly for a date with someone we love. Being remembered is flattering; being researched is even more so. Feeling that our secrets—even the relatively innocuous ones—are in someone else's memory is also subtly intimidating. Consider all the cultures which make a fetish of concealing such information as the true names of their tribe members. Clearly, we're inclined to attribute power to those in the know.

GET THE SMALL DETAILS RIGHT

Another important aspect of selling yourself effectively is to really care about all the small niceties that gradually accumulate into a truly winning image. My super-organized associate, for example, has devised phone policies that highlight his image of relentless reliability:

• He makes all calls at the exact hour and time he promised—*and not one minute later*. If the recipient of his call isn't in, he negotiates a new calling appointment with the screener and promptly enters it on his daily schedule.

• He schedules same-day call-backs by himself or his assistant to everyone who calls his office during his absence, whether he knows them or not.

• He's never caught by surprise if a tardy call-back comes in for him. By keeping his contact files next to the phone, he's able to instantly refresh himself as to the topic of the original call as he greets the caller.

• He's instructed his assistant to unfailingly do two things: pick up all calls by the second ring and banish the words "I don't know" from her vocabulary.

• When he receives a call, he lets the other person hang up first. Sometimes, he finds, a last-minute thought can translate into an additional sale or lead for new business.

• In follow-up calls to new contacts, he never assumes that his name or business will evoke instant recollection. Instead, he tactfully reintroduces himself with a few vivid words.

• Since his first name is a common one, he always identifies himself by his full name, even to intimates, to avoid momentary confusion. If he's leaving a message on an answering machine, he also spells his name and repeats his number slowly enough so that the other person can write it down without having to replay the tape a second time.

• Once someone has bought from him, he schedules a call a few weeks later to thank them for the order and to inquire how they like the materials he's supplied.

• He takes his assistant into his confidence by providing her with a weekly list of those he'd most like to hear from. Should one of these desirable callers get in touch, he's instructed her to convey an image of both courtesy and importance by saying, "He's quite busy right now, but I know he's eager to speak with *you* regarding the XYZ project. I'll let him know right away that you're on the line."

ADD A PERSONAL TOUCH

It's possible to be *too* businesslike on the telephone. While a just-the-facts approach is fine on the first call, in subsequent calls a touch of friendliness advances the relationship and helps create rapport. If you seem receptive to such overtures, many of your associates will *want* to reveal themselves with conversational clues as to their favorite activities, particular interests and other personal preoccupations. Responding to such signals with an appropriate—but not intrusive—interest shows that you don't just see the other person as a source of potential income for yourself but as a genuinely *valued* associate.

Even such a minor item as an associate's reference to his or her vacation plans is a seed of intimacy that can be cultivated in future interactions. You might send her an article you happen to see about that particular locale, ask during your next call if she enjoyed the trip or suggest a restaurant that your family enjoyed when you were there. Similarly, if he's out sick when you call, a little courteous concern from you will be appreciated when he returns to work. (But do avoid the temptation to regale him with your own medical woes, past or present.) Such gestures are warm, but don't invade the other person's privacy.

Confiding a less-than-intimate detail or two about yourself can also stimulate rapport—but select such confessions with care. You'll want to avoid giving the message, directly or indirectly, that you have any financial, romantic or personal difficulties of any kind (even if you do). Letting it be thought that you have problems outside of the office invites scrutiny of just how well you're doing in the office. Instead, accentuate the positive: You might do a little discreet bragging about your daughter's making the dean's list, your son's summer internship at a prestigious organization or your spouse's promotion. Having an accomplished family reflects well upon you, as do interesting references to your hobbies, recreation and entertainment, travel and reading material. You show yourself to be a well-rounded person, both on and off the job.

A little gift or token may be appropriate in some industries. Twice a year I am pleasantly reminded of the name of my insurance agent—it appears as the signature on the attractive birthday and holiday cards he unfailingly sends me. I've also had authors who sent me flowers to celebrate having joined my clientele or having sold their first book—which made me feel a warm (although in some cases, rather short-lived) glow about our blossoming association.

Information is another gift that is always appreciated. A salesman of home security systems always follows up his initial phone call to a homeowner by mailing him an informative booklet he's written on fire prevention tactics—even if the prospect has turned him down. A wedding consultant has assembled a photocopied packet of interesting articles about various aspects of planning a wedding, which she gives to each couple who telephones to inquire about engaging her services; while a real estate agent gives her clients an annotated list of local restaurants—observing in a covering note that she personally visited and enjoyed each one.

Being generous with your favors—even if you have no immediate expectation of getting something back—can be a sound investment in future goodwill. Acquaintances often ask me for leads to good jobs in publishing—either for themselves, or more frequently, for their recently graduated children. As a result, I've cultivated an ear for job opportunities and usually have heard about an opening or two that might be appropriate. As a result, some of those I helped out several years ago are now in a position to help me—I recently made a sale to one of my former protégés.

ADVERTISE YOUR ACCOMPLISHMENTS

Occasionally tooting your own horn—softly, of course—does definitely attract favorable attention. But how do you script advertisements for yourself that sell subtly yet compellingly?

Your first step, say advertising experts Al Reis and Jack Trout, authors of *Positioning: The Battle for Your Mind,* is to realize that there are only so many ladders into the other person's mind that a new idea can climb and that the rungs of most of them are already full of competing information. That's why it's crucial to zero in on a single catchy concept with riflelike precision, rather than blast away with multiple messages in the hope of hitting a vital spot somewhere.

Here are some approaches to finding that psychic nerve:

• **Try judicious name-dropping.** A celebrity endorsement—even if it's from someone whose renown only extends within your own industry—never hurts business. Elizabeth Tener, who's enjoyed considerable success at self-marketing, both in the professional and romantic arenas—she's the author of *Getting Personal: Finding that Special Someone Through the Classifieds* and she's a widely published business writer—likes to deftly weave the names of her regular customers into phone pitches to new editors. To convey the message that she enjoys excellent industry contacts and is much-sought-after, she'll say something like, "When I was speaking the other day with X [a top editor at a major magazine] about a piece I just did for her, it struck me that a related article on this topic would be relevant to *your* readers."

It's also helpful to inform new contacts about any previous successes you've had with others at their firm. Seven of my most successful clients all published their books with the same large publishing house—but different editors handled each of these deals. When I find myself dealing with a newcomer to this firm, I'll work the roll call of these Magnificent Seven titles into the conversation as naturally as possible—thus firmly establishing my agenting credentials.

• **Trade on your company's clout.** Bask in the reflected glory of any successes your company has achieved recently. While too much boasting about yourself will turn off others, a zestful brag or two about your *company* shows you to be admirably loyal and a good team player. It's a sign of character to put the company's cachet before your own—and a superior sales strategy, should your company have already established its good name with the prospect while you are still an unknown entity to him.

If your firm is a large one, you'll increase your stature by association. Emphasize the vast resources that stand behind you, and show the person how you can connect him to additional services that he—not necessarily you—will profit from. Or, if the firm is small or newly established, stress its stellar track record in going that extra mile to deliver satisfaction. The better you make the company look, the better you'll look—because they had the good judgment to engage *you* as one of their ambassadors.

• **They'll believe it when they see it in print.** Good publicity helps you get established quickly. Consider writing an article for your trade magazine (for free if necessary) or offer it the opportunity to reprint any speeches you happen to make. Often these publications are starving for good material by insiders, making these markets easier to crack than most aspiring authors anticipate.

Consider also proposing yourself as a speaker at professional conferences (the earlier you make your move, the more likely you are to get on the calendar) or as an instructor on your field at a local adult education center. Hold a seminar of your own for others in the industry; make sure to send relevant details in a press release directly to industry publications.

• **Carve your niche with a stream of minor accomplishments.** A Madison Avenue technique you can borrow is to plot your campaign around several vignettes that reinforce the same basic idea. In one call, you might tell an amusing, but not indiscreet, anecdote about a recent sale you made; in another, mention some notable you've dealt with recently; and in a third, refer offhandedly to some upgrade in your lifestyle, with a light remark about your new boat, say.

It's important as you do this to have the appropriate lift and energy to your voice if you're to give the impression that you're on a roll lately. Avoid the temptation to bludgeon others with the message of how busy and successful you are, though, lest you arouse anxieties that *their* project is a low priority item with you. Make it clear that at least part of your current excitement is due to the thrilling potential you see in working with them.

• **Remove the string from failure.** If you're getting back in touch with someone who failed to grab the last deal you had to offer, a bit of image-restoration may be in order. Most of us have a mental category labeled "the big ones that got away," where we ruefully file memories of missed opportunities of the past. So it makes sense where possible to vividly demonstrate that your previous offering was another of these bad judgment calls on your prospect's part.

Since you don't want to make him or her defensive about it, you might gracefully mention how well another prominent company has done with the product or service or an unexpected bonus that some other customer has realized from the transaction. Don't go on to complete the analogy with any reference to the prospect's own situation or needs. If the conclusion fits, he or she will recognize it privately, and the correct selling climate will be established.

• **You can live almost forever on one success—if it's really spectacular.** Although Andy Warhol once said that in the future everyone will be world famous for fifteen minutes, I've known a number of people who've successfully parlayed fifteen minutes of long-past fame into twenty years—or more—of excellent income. The patina of time can also enhance less-than-stellar success into something grander and more romantic—especially when the people you speak with are only hearing *your* side of the story.

The notable achievement that characterizes you need not even be your own. One businessman of my acquaintance enjoys a giant reputation and substantial earnings because of a remarkable coup once pulled off by an individual of the same name—his recently retired father. Like father, like son, clients and customers reason—and my associate does his best to capitalize on the magic and mystique of the name and image he's inherited.

• **A magnificent scheme makes you memorable.** Still waiting in the wings for your fifteen minutes in the limelight? The ability to *think* big adds star quality to your phone presence—and raises the even more dramatic possibility that your scheme will actually succeed. It's exhilarating to imagine how a small deal could be transformed into a giant one or what sort of innovative venture might be worked out between you and your phone contacts. Even if your initial proposal doesn't take, a connection between you and exciting, major projects has been created in their minds. They will want to recapture the thrills—and may come back to you with an idea of theirs or put you in touch with another opportunity.

• **Dazzle them with dollar signs.** Another essential ingredient of effective advertising is to create an image based upon price. There are two workable approaches: the irresistible bargain or the outrageous luxury. To pull off either successfully, you need the ability to mention large sums of money unblushingly—and to convey total conviction that you deserve them. For example, I was once able to persuade a client of mine that paying me two thousand dollars to make a ten-minute phone call on her behalf was an unbeatable price. Why? Because I truly believed—and still do—that what she was buying wasn't ten minutes of my time but the twelve years I'd devoted to learning who to call and what to say in this type of negotiation.

PACKAGING YOURSELF FOR EMPLOYMENT

Although the standard employment advice emphasizes job hunting via mail, selling your job skills by telephone offers a number of advantages. Even the most power-packed cover letter and resume can languish on the desk of someone without decision-making power, while a phone call lets you target your pitch to the person who holds hiring authority. And even if your letter does reach the proper person—and gets read—the written word just doesn't convey your personality with the same warmth and vitality as a smoothly handled phone presentation. Best of all, a "telesearch" offers the potential gratification of immediate results—a few words in the right ear, and you could be scheduling a next-day interview appointment.

Here are some selling strategies recommended by recruiters:

• **Be superorganized.** Before phoning, assemble several pens, your appointment calendar and your list of the names, numbers and personnel contacts at the prospective employers you'll be calling that day. Block out enough time to make all your calls in rapid sequence—the momentum you establish is likely to be reflected in an increasingly polished presentation. That's why you should open with the *last*-choice employers—you'll be fully psyched by the time you get to the prime candidates.

• **Be first on the line.** Start your calling as early in the day as possible. The interviewer will be rested and alert, letting you make a better impression than when he's numb from fielding all the other calls about the job. Similarly, it's best to call at the beginning of the week, before his schedule—or the job—has been filled. Friday morning can also be a good time; not only will you beat next week's competition, but the interviewer is apt to be in a receptive mood now that he is happily anticipating the weekend.

• **Hit the highlights.** Since your objective should be to sell the interview, rather than attempt to get hired on the spot or to screen the company, a good presentation should stress *one* key benefit of hiring you, not your entire resume. Addressing the other person by name (get it from the ad or the receptionist), your message might be something like this: "Mr. Lewis, this is

Alana Hopeful. I have five years' experience in software sales and would like to arrange an appointment tomorrow to discuss the possibility of working with you. Would ten o'clock be convenient or would you prefer two o'clock?"

This approach, like all good sales pitches, assumes the sale and focuses on nailing down the order. You've avoided the weak position of asking if the job is still open—which can sound as if you don't really expect to get it—while making a negative answer difficult. Should the choice of appointments be rejected, your fallback position is to suggest some times the following day.

• **Prepare winning replies to objections.** Anticipate that some of your prospects will offer such excuses as "I'm too busy"; "Send me your resume"; "Call personnel"; "We've already conducted several interviews, and will make our selections from those"; and "We're looking for someone more qualified." All of these can be countered with snappy one-liners, followed by a renewed request for an appointment: "I would send my resume, but I believe that you'd get an even better idea of the qualities and experience that I'd bring to the job if we met briefly in person. How's tomorrow afternoon?"

• **Confirm as you close.** Once you've gotten the appointment, wind up the call quickly by thanking the person and repeating the salient details back for confirmation: "I'll look forward to seeing you at nine on Wednesday, the twenty-seventh."

RESELLING YOURSELF

Is the romance over as soon as you've made the sale or gotten your immediate objective accomplished? Here are ten good reasons *not* to love and leave your telephone contacts:
• #1. Investing a few minutes in a stroking call—where

no overt business deal is discussed—can prevent costly customer defections to more ardent competitors. You'll also be able to avert having a minor misunderstanding fester into a major problem.

• #2. You won't lose sales during the cooling-off period, when the customer temporarily doubts the wisdom of his buying decision. By contacting him during this vulnerable period—perhaps to thank him for the order or to give some helpful additional information, you prolong the honeymoon.

• #3. Now that he or she's in the buying mood, keeping in touch might let you capitalize on additional needs that occur to the other person after the original sale. You may also glean some tidbits about his buying cycles or future needs that will allow you to pinpoint the best time for your next sales call.

• #4. You increase your credibility by showing that you're in business for the long term. He or she recognizes that this transaction isn't just a one-time occurrence, but rather that you can be counted upon both now and in the future.

• #5. By keeping yourself in the forefront of his or her mind, you're in a good position to collect any leads or referrals that the other person may generate.

• #6. By delivering periodic progress reports, if indicated, the other person never asks him- or herself, "What has he done for me lately?" In service-oriented businesses, clients may not realize just how much behind-the-scenes work you are actually doing on their behalf unless you tell them regularly.

• #7. By increasing your associate's exposure to you and your services, he or she's inspired to think of other ways to exploit this new connection that you may have overlooked. He's also more likely to mention your attentive attitude to others, gaining you valuable word of mouth publicity from those who matter.

• #8. You vividly impart to the other person the idea that he or she is special, and you can tailor mini-presentations of good new opportunities around this concept. You'll also send the message that special attention can be expected if he or she has an out-of-the-ordinary need in the future.

• #9. Should you happen to find yourself in the unfortunate position of having to deliver some bad news—the merchandise is going to be late or the investment has proved less profitable than anticipated—you'll have a stockpile of previously stored good feelings and trust to draw upon when you deliver the bad tidings.

• #10. By linking your fortune with that of your new associate, you can watch your success grow along with his. Not only can a small account blossom into a large one over time, but establishing a group of regular, reliable customers—both small and large—is an excellent foundation to build upon in the future.

10

WINNING THROUGH NEGOTIATION

On Wall Street, Gertrude Stein once said, the money remains the same, it's merely the pockets that change. A similar remark could be made about negotiation, except that the truly skilled practitioner sometimes can arrange the transfers between pockets so artfully that both parties conclude the discussion cheerfully convinced that the pocket that now has the extra jingle to it is *theirs*.

As an agent, I have often found that the ring of my phone might well herald the ring of my cash register, with an editor calling to make an offer for rights to one of my client's books. While clients may consider this the beginning of the bargaining, my *real* negotiations may have been launched even before their particular project was conceived or typed. Just as any business call you make contains a hidden sales pitch—for yourself—so also does each telephone transaction between you and potential buyers or sellers contain the seeds of incipient negotiation.

STARTING FROM STRENGTH

As the saying goes, "Nothing succeeds like success," which is why your attention to image-building will pay off in negotiation. If you let your opponent get the scent of blood—by projecting an air of weakness or hunger—you'll arouse his killer instincts in the forthcoming battle of wits. When you offer him a superbly equipped and powerful adversary in yourself, he'll positively relish the competitive challenge. Give him what he wants—a good time, the thrill of the chase, an opportunity to demonstrate his financial clout and gain emotional gratification—and he'll give you what you want—*money*. Paradoxically, the less he thinks you need his deal, the more he'll work to overcome your resistance.

Ideally, you should start establishing a powerful position as soon as you begin any new business relationship. Since the right intelligence about the opponent will arm your negotiating points with added impact, use preliminary discussions as opportunities to glean potentially valuable clues as to the other person's direct needs and psychological hot buttons. Since no real commitment has been made—or demanded—at this point, the other party is apt to be relatively relaxed—and, perhaps, off guard. Through his or her immediate reactions and unstudied remarks, you may sense how hungry he or she really is as well as learning specific facts that will enhance your negotiating efforts.

A sports promoter, for example, often asks during the initial discussion of a possible celebrity endorsement just how many units of the item the firm expects to sell. The company's representative will often inflate the figures because he subconsciously wants to inflate his own importance and success. Once mellowed by these pleasant reflections, he may well elaborate on the plans the firm has for the product, indirectly revealing just how hungry he is for the deal. The sports promoter can then use this information later as a negotiating point for his client—arguing that the high anticipated sales volume the customer has indicated justifies the high price the promoter's now asking.

Naturally, the canny negotiator can also use the initial phone discussion to plant advantageous information in the other person's mind. If you consider yourself to be offering a hot property of some sort, you can create the right psychological climate by using words like "major" and "big," by making analogies with other large deals you or the other person has participated in or is familiar with and by emphasizing your own enthusiasm and confidence in the idea. While buyers naturally do expect hyperbole from sellers, a *genuine* sense of excitement can be quite contagious. Stress also that you are only looking for a *serious* buyer or a *serious* offer. Seriousness and megabucks are concepts that are intimately linked in every businessperson's psyche.

Beware of similar tactics from your opponent, however. One business broker I know received several calls from an interested prospect about a distributorship he was representing. The buyer invariably made dark comments about the general resistance to the idea within his company and the uphill battle he was waging on the broker's behalf. Before ending each conversation, the buyer would inform the seller that there was the "faintest possibility" of a "very modest offer." The inexperienced broker began to feel that he would be lucky to realize $100,000, though he had earlier valued the business at $250,000. When the buyer finally presented him with a big of $150,000, it seemed almost like a gift. Poorer, but wiser, this broker now says, "I should have pressed for the $250,000."

In my work, I encountered an editor who achieved much the same effect on me with just *three* sentences. Her opening remark was, "I love the book." Visions of dollar signs immediately danced through my head. She continued with, "How much do you want?" More dollar signs joined the mental chorus line, as I debated how much to hold her up for. Before I could reply, however, she added a final salvo: "No, that is too much." Although I was amused by this ploy in retrospect, at the time her technique of telepathic negotiation did work—by getting me to bargain *myself* downward.

HIDDEN SOURCES OF POWER

The power of precedents established in previous negotiations can work for—or against—you in the current one. Recently I was hired by several writers whose previous agent had retired. Their contracts—all with the same publisher—testified that, alas, their former representative was no demon negotiator. Since the price an author has received for his or her previous book is often a basis for negotiating subsequent sales, I realized that unless I found different precedents to evoke, these orphaned authors would have a hard time getting more than their accustomed mite. Looking over the previous deals I'd made with this publisher, I located a set of "comparables" from my clientele—and used their contracts to embarrass this editor into bringing my new clients' advances into the twentieth century.

The existence of competing buyers or sellers—or the threat of approaching such individuals—will also improve your negotiating posture, since it shows that you have *options*. I once made a nice sale with what I call the "buyer-in-the-bush" ploy. Although I usually offer most of my projects simultaneously to all likely publishers in the hope of inciting an auction, I decided to try out this one on the best candidate. As I had hoped, she soon telephoned to express strong interest. I told her that I was delighted, and said that after I'd shown it to the other fifteen buyers I was about to approach, we'd chat again. With a note of alarm in her voice, she said she'd spare me the effort—I could expect her bid later in the day. Forty-five minutes later, my fifteen hypothetical buyers were battling her offer-in-the-hand until she hit upon my client's magic number.

Learning the details of other person's timetable—without revealing yours—gives you additional leverage. In another of my negotiations, a publisher revealed that he passionately hoped to put this particular book on his next list. With this ammunition, I was able to get him to raise his price several times—despite a complete absence of competing offers—by repeatedly informing him that my client, a highly successful executive, had expected more money and was therefore "thinking things over." As the publisher became more and more frustrated with these delays, he broke down and asked me just how much it would take to get the client to stop thinking and start writing. I named my most optimistic figure and promised that the client would be typing page one early the next morning should we cut a deal today. The impatient publisher screamed, "At that price, I expect him at work *this afternoon!*"

Being able to defer instant gratification definitely pays off. A businesswoman I know spent several years in on-and-off negotiations to end a rather tedious lawsuit that had been brought against her company. Unexpectedly, the opposing lawyer offered an extremely attractive resolution to the problem. Although her first impulse was to snap at the bait before it was withdrawn, she was wise enough to stall while she and her lawyers quickly researched the idea. As a result, she was able to call back the following day to propose an even more advantageous settlement plan, bolstered by an impressive array of facts and citations to justify it. She calculates that she saved over twenty thousand dollars from that overnight delay.

Another easily acquired source of power is the ability to be politely persistent. A lawyer replies to all initial negotiating points with one of two replies: "I can live with that" or "Let's get back to that one later." The first response, in his opinion, suggests appropriately reluctant agreement, while the second puts off the debate on unappealing points while he gets the other party "a little bit pregnant" by establishing areas of mutual agreement. In subsequent discussions, he systematically chips away at each obstacle with tiny changes of position, addressing all counterarguments with his two stock replies. Nearly always, he's able to sculpt a satisfactory agreement with a few phone calls.

Sometimes, paradoxically, *not* having much power can work to your advantage in negotiation. As an agent, I'm in a position to extract concessions and commitments from the buyers with whom I deal without actually having the authority to commit my clients to accepting any of these arrangements. This provides two good opportunities to negotiate each point— first to upgrade the offer before presenting it to the client with remarks like, "I'm sure she'll never go for that"; then to return to the fray with new arguments from the client. Also, should it seem desirable to stall—perhaps in anticipation of a better offer from someone else—it's easy enough to contrive some difficulty in contacting the client, while continuing to press for additional concessions or a better price.

Even if you are the ultimate authority, it's not always wise to admit it to the opponent. In his book, *What They Don't Teach You About Business at Harvard Business School,* entrepreneur Mark H. McCormack writes, "In any new business situation, when someone tells me, 'I'm the decision maker around here' and I have reason to believe this is true, my lips start to smack. He has already cut off his first line of defense." Instead, keep a shadowy figure in the background—a boss, partner, agent, lawyer, spouse—and withdraw to consult him or her whenever the going seems to be getting tough. You'll gain time to recoup—and possibly some good advice from the associate as well.

STREET-SMART STRATEGIES

Money talks, but what's it really saying during a negotiation? Whether you're buying or selling, most of its whispers have to do with fear and greed: every seller secretly imagines him- or herself trading away Manhattan for twenty-four dollars worth of trinkets, while the buyer darkly envisions the sure thing he hopes to acquire turning out to be the Edsel of the '80s. At the same time, there's the thrilling fantasy of finding ourselves on the *other* end of these deals. The uncertainty of the outcome is what makes negotiation so exciting—and challenging.

Here's how to speak softly and carry a big negotiating stick:

• **Start with the bottom line.** Would-be authors often ask me a question like: "What size advance could you get from a publisher for a book on motherhood?" My usual reply is, "Somewhere between nothing and four-and-a-half million."—a rather safe bet since the figure of $4.5 million represents publishing's current record advance. The trickier question is to define the appropriate price range for a particular author's work, since each book is a unique "product."

Rather than try to calculate a novel or nonfiction book's dollar value in some abstract sense, the most successful approach, I've found, is to *reverse* my thinking and evaluate it from the other person's perspective. Not only does this tip you off to their likely bargaining points—and suggest possible strategies to counter them—but it lets you figure in such intangibles as the "romance" factor. Perhaps the project has taken on some personal significance to the editor, has a glamour and cachet the company hopes will rub off on the rest of its list or is the kind of big buy that will attract the major offerings of the most important sellers.

Once you've settled upon the high and low ends of "how much," it's also useful to decide in advance what trade-offs you are willing to make (if necessary) to get your price. Books have a variety of rights, such as magazine excerpts, full adaptations and foreign translations, that are sometimes given to the buyer and sometimes reserved by the seller. Thus, a price must also be put on these aspects of the package prior to negotiation— along with more complex deal points such as a multibook contract, exclusive rights to a particular pen name and other sweeteners that might be thrown in for the right price.

• **Be slow to name your price.** Your control of the negotiations will be enhanced if you let the other person be the first to talk about numbers and terms. You'll gain insight into just which ballpark he's playing in—perhaps a more upscale one than you'd hoped for—while keeping your own thinking concealed. And, depending on your side of the table, you gain the advantage of working upward or downward from his figures.

A hypothetical question or two can be quite informative. If you are buying, you might try an opening move along the lines of: "This sounds like something we might be interested in exploring further. If we were to come in with a preemptive bid, what would it take to walk away with it?" A cagy seller could then probe for more information with a hypothetical question of his own: "Well, it would depend on the structure of the deal. If we were to offer you X rights, how much do you think that might be worth?"

• **Pick numbers with sex appeal.** When you do reveal your ideas on price or terms, an alluring presentation helps. You might try an analogy with a previous successful deal: "I see this as quite similar to X, which as you may know, sold for $Y. Of course that was last year, and X didn't have features A and

B . . ." Success by association is often enough to get the other person thinking at a higher level in pricing the current project.

Another point to keep in mind is that round numbers, such as $100,000, seem to beg for negotiation, while an odd number like $97,500, has a more finely calculated ring—as if you've toted up each element of the deal with great precision. Also, there's the psychological factor of being just under six figures that still creates the illusion of a bargain.

• **Allow an easy victory or two.** A well-structured game plan should include a few "throwaway" points that the opponent is apt to reject. After he's won a few in the early rounds, he'll not only feel that he can afford to be generous later on, but he may begin to imagine that he actually *owes* you a corresponding number of "yeses" for those "nos" he's managed to chalk up on his side.

Your giveaways will be more effective if you present them as if they were of equal importance to your other points. Let the opponent sense that you're not serious about these deal items, and you'll devalue the psychological debt that you're accumulating or risk having the strategy unravel altogether. Instead, seem a bit disappointed at being outsmarted by his shrewd negotiating; you might laugh and say, "Well, it was worth a try" or "I was afraid you'd say that."

• **Offer convenient cues.** Since your opponent will be intent on trying to "read" the hidden messages in what you say, why not slip him or her some obvious clues? For example, let's say that during the negotiation you make this series of offers: $17,500; $20,000; $22,000; $23,500; $24,500—presenting each new bid with increasing hesitation. The other person need not be a mathematical genius to figure that your next bid will probably be $25,000 and to infer from the decreasing increments of your offers that this represents your top price.

But does it? A bidding strategy like this could well be a clever diversion to keep the opponent from suspecting that you'd really go to $35,000 or even higher if you thought it necessary. What makes this type of cueing so effective is that the other person suggests the desired idea to *himself*, which automatically makes it seem much more credible than any explicit statement from you, which he'll immediately discount as a possible ploy.

• **Piggyback on his ideas.** Effective negotiation is somewhat like the cynic's definition of love: a state of cooperative egotism. That's why you'll find it a lot easier to sell the other person on his own ideas—modified, of course, to suit *your* goals as well— than to persuade him to adopt some new, and possibly alien, approach. Our first reaction to novelty, especially in a negotiation, is suspicion; while even a faint echo of our own earlier sentiments or arguments has a reassuringly familiar ring.

Whenever feasible, present your negotiating points as logical developments of the other person's previous suggestions, or as solutions to objections *he's* identified. Buttress your arguments with the facts and opinions you've solicited from him during your earlier discussions to illustrate how well your plan fits his self-interest.

Not only will this approach help the other person's needs and priorities in an appealing way but you'll gain the tactical advantage of having concealed your own. We tend to assume that the other person will place equal weight on the points we consider most important—and should this *not* be the case, you'll be in a position to trade a minor (from your perspective) concession for a far more valuable one from your opponent.

• **Avoid macho ego contests.** Too confrontational an attitude will actually damage your odds of achieving the most advantageous deal—or in getting a deal at all. I once represented a writer who was so determined not to lose by conceding a single point to his publisher that he lost a profitable deal over *three* words in his contract—none of which had any measurable impact on his potential earnings from the book.

Similarly, ultratough tactics can backfire. Issuing rigid deadlines, take-it-or-leave-it ultimatums and throwing around words like "deal-breaker" and "nonnegotiable" usually succeed only in provoking retaliatory strikes from the other person. Or worse still, he might opt for the "or else" half of your threat—and then what? Instead try a "soft" ultimatum: "I appreciate your position, but $X is the maximum I've been authorized to spend on this item. What do you suggest we do about it?"

• **Use emotion creatively.** Recently I dropped into the office of a lawyer I know and overheard him screaming furiously into his telephone, apparently in response to some outrageous negotiating point raised by the other person. Turning to me—the volume of his outburst rising steadily—he gave a friendly wink, as if to say, "Don't take any of this too seriously, I'm just playing the game."

This struck me as the correct attitude to bring into a heated negotiation. Genuinely losing control of oneself can often mean losing control of the negotiations, because you're not acting with logic, but *reacting* viscerally. That's why an emotional outburst from the opponent can represent an opportunity: Give him a chance to save face and feel back in control, and he's sure to reward you accordingly.

• **Know when to bite your tongue.** As P. T. Barnum once said, "There's a sucker born every minute." While his calculations seem a bit inflated in my experience, once in a while you'll spot some monumental bit of stupidity on the part of the opponent. Perhaps his initial offer is beyond your wildest dreams of avarice, or he makes you a gift of some prized point without asking for anything substantial in return. That's when silence really is golden—a blurted exclamation is almost certainly an expensive error.

If you lack a perfect poker face, the phone is an ideal mask. Anytime you find yourself startled, or caught off guard, a slow mental count of ten will allow you time to collect your thoughts without revealing them through body language. And should you feel that additional reflection is required, there's always the excuse of an urgent call on the other line or the more desperate tactic of "accidentally" disconnecting yourself (best to do when *you* are in the midst of speaking).

• **Don't go for the last ounce of flesh.** I was once fortunate enough to find myself negotiating with an inexperienced movie producer who proved to be woefully ignorant of the standard terms of television contracts. Although I did take advantage of him—who wouldn't—I was generous enough to educate him about a few minor points that were more in his interest than mine. A year or so later, he'd risen to some prominence in the industry, and I called him about another project. By now, he was savvy enough to realize how I'd outsmarted him—and informed me in an amused but slightly threatening way that I wouldn't find him such an easy mark in the future.

What I realized was that most of us don't really mind being outsmarted by a clever adversary as long it doesn't hurt too much. Leave them with something and they'll eventually appreciate the rather expensive lesson they've learned; strip them totally bare and they'll be out for your blood next time.

• **Bluff a bit, but don't lie.** Ethical standards do vary from industry to industry. A buyer for a large department store told me that she frequently encounters dishonesty from sellers. "It's really a cutthroat business," she says. "Negotiating with a vendor is like doing a crossword puzzle—nothing is out in the open, everything is in code. I hate to say it, but there's a lot of out-and-out lying, which makes it impossible to determine where the opposition really stands . . . Of course, I happen to be a freak for crossword puzzles, and unraveling the untruths is what makes negotiation so interesting."

The others I interviewed took a different view. They agreed that it's ethical to keep certain information confidential—it's the job of the other side to dig up publicly available facts that could affect price—such as the existence of competing projects already in production at other firms. Furthermore, the consensus was that a negotiator has no obligation to reveal the amounts of other offers or who made them. However, I heard several stories about individuals who crossed the line between appropriate secrecy and dishonesty—by taking bids "off the wall" from nonexistent competitors, for example—*and were found out to their dishonor*.

• **Startle them with honesty.** Since your opponent is going to suspect everything you do of being some sort of ploy, perhaps the ultimate strategem is honesty. Competition can be turned to a more collaborative process once the appropriate atmosphere of mutual respect has been established by well-timed candor. When the deal is almost hammered out—and the other person feels that he now has a substantial investment in its success—it might be the right moment to say, "My client's absolutely obsessive about royalty rates. Can't you throw in . . .?"

• **Be the caller, not the called.** Answer the phone during a negotiation and you're already in a defensive position. Your opponent has the facts and figures in front of him and has marshalled some arguments, while you may be scanning the daily paper or attending to some other business. Even if you have lightning mental reflexes, there's still an important loss of initiative. Recapture it by offering a graceful exit line—that important meeting or overseas call that just can't wait—and return the call when *you're* primed for success.

Maintain this advantageous position after the negotiation by offering to be the one to confirm it in writing. Your memo of agreement will quite naturally be expressed in *your* terms, with the elaborations or definitions you consider most helpful and will serve as a basis for future revisions or expanded contracts. Making a habit of this after any important telephone transaction will not only reinforce your businesslike image but avoid the problem that Sam Goldwyn defined so vividly: "An oral agreement isn't worth the paper it's written on."

GETTING OFF THE HOOK

It's said that the Chinese use the same ideogram to represent the words "danger" and "opportunity." In business life, problems can fall on either side of this spectrum—handle them poorly and there's the danger of irreparably damaging a valued relationship with an associate or a customer; resolve them satisfactorily, and there's the opportunity to gain increased trust and goodwill from others. While a winning image and professional style do inspire confidence in you, your success at coping with a challenge *proves* that you really do have the right stuff.

Troublesome calls are also educational opportunities, in that they alert you to areas of weakness in your business approach. A complaint, for example, could expose the need for improvements in your product or service or methods of doing business. By telling of his dissatisfaction, the caller is doing you a disguised favor; others may have noticed the same deficiency and have simply moved their business elsewhere—saying nothing to you while spreading negative word-of-mouth to others.

138

USING YOUR PHONE TO PREVENT PROBLEMS

Not only does your phone offer your customers and associates a chance to get instant results when a complaint or misunderstanding arises, but with the right tactics you can sometimes *prevent* such problems from occurring in the first place. Contacting those with whom you are conducting any major transaction periodically allows you to pass along information about the action you have taken or will be taking on their behalf, alert them to unavoidable delays, correct misunderstandings and demonstrate your overall concern with the smooth completion of the arrangements. Equally vital in today's highly competitive environment are follow-up calls *after* the deal is done—a quick, economical way of ferreting out dissatisfaction and maintaining goodwill.

Since it's impossible to predict exactly when a customer might have a problem, organizing a telephone support system allows you to provide the speediest service at the lowest cost. At Coefficient Systems Corporation, a computer software firm, Robert Saft, their director of technical support services, finds that 85 percent of customer questions or problems can be resolved during a single phone call. "Although the problem, frequently, isn't with our product at all, but results from the customer's unfamiliarity with the operating system on his particular computer, or misunderstanding about the nature of his hardware, I'll still spend the time to talk them through the procedure, and get our product up and running."

The advantages of offering telephone service of this type, observes Saft, include fewer costly field visits to service your customers, an expanded support system for geographically distant consumers and the ability to provide instant gratification to the customer by giving him back the use of his equipment immediately. Thus, everyone's time and money is saved, and a minor problem isn't allowed to fester into a major grievance that might result in the loss of repeat business from that account.

Saft has some suggestions for those who are thinking of setting up a similar system:

• **Adopt a supportive attitude.** "It's hard to be patient when the customer asks a question that he could easily answer if he'd just bother to read the manual that accompanies the product, but it's vital to remember that support is part of what he's buying when he places an order with you," says Saft.

• **Handle the call with professionalism and competence.** The customer must immediately feel that he's reached a technically informed individual. The person who handles the call must be aware that the customer may give erroneous information about his equipment or lack the vocabulary to adequately describe exactly what he's done or wishes to do. Therefore, he must be quizzed diplomatically in some cases or given the proper instructions slowly and in an easy-to-understand wording. It's better to be *too* simple than to assume too much sophistication.

Preparing a "bible" of answers to the more frequently asked questions or common problems lets support staffers respond in the most consistent and complete manner. It's especially useful when step-by-step diagnostic procedures are advised or complex technical instructions given.

• **Keep response time down.** A technical problem, such as those Saft handles, may have put the customer's whole business on hold—so realize that in the caller's mind the meter has started ticking from the moment he's placed the call. Being shuffled from person to person or department to department compounds the problem, as do slow or hesitant answers. If, for some reason, the problem transcends normal support procedures, arrange a return call from a higher-up in the firm—as rapidly as possible.

• **Consider a WATS line.** Should you handle a large volume of out-of-town business, you may find that dissatisfied customers are reluctant to call you at their own expense—feeling that paying for the call adds insult to injury. At a smaller company, you may find it thriftier to encourage collect calls; but at a larger firm the more cost-effective and appealing solution can be to promote toll free calling from your customers via an incoming WATS (Wide Area Telephone Service) line. These can either be national or restricted to a smaller area, such as your state.

Another method of advertising your accessibility is to give out a special number, such as your direct dialing number, night line or even your home number to favored associates. Chances are that you'll get relatively few calls yet make a most favorable impression about your commitment to capturing— and retaining—the other person's goodwill and future business. Being a little bit ceremonial about handing out the number adds to its cachet and makes the customer or associate feel special.

YOU ACTION LINE FOR COMPLAINTS

Since even the best-run office of business will invariably receive some complaining calls, you'll save time—and possibly a profitable account—by preparing some fire-fighting tactics in advance. Here's how:

Step One: Be part of the solution, not of the problem. Though it's only natural to feel defensive when your product, service or overall competence is questioned, a confrontational stance will only exacerbate the problem. Avoid inflammatory remarks like:

"Are you claiming that . . .?" Words like "claim," "state," and "allege" are offensive because they are obvious attacks on the other person's credibility and give him a new grievance beyond the initial complaint.

"I don't see what you expect me to do about it." The right attitude is that the buck *does* stop here—with you—or that you will explain exactly why the call should be referred to someone else within the organization.

"I've been here ten years, and no one's ever complained about it before." Here the other person is made to feel that he's not only injured, but unlucky as well—or that you're being deceptive. Furthermore, characterizing his criticism as a "complaint" makes it sound as if he's whining or being disagreeable. It's better to refer to "the misunderstanding" or "your experience."

Step Two: Project an empathic attitude. Even if the caller seems upset or angry, it's important to realize that *you are not the target*—the problem is. Some of us find it hard to make even the most justified complaint without whipping ourselves up into an a combative mood. To defuse the tension, start by expressing your sympathy: "I'm sorry to hear of this" or "I can appreciate your concern about this." Neutral but soothing phrases like this let the other person know that he or she's reached an understanding—and potentially helpful—ally.

Giving the other person your name and title, should he or she not have asked for you specifically, increases rapport by showing that you're taking responsibility for the matter personally. It is also likely to decrease any hostility from the caller, since it's easier to be furious with a faceless bureaucracy and the unfamiliar voice representing it than with a real, breathing person with a name and personality.

Step Three: Determine the facts. Since the complainer may be overwrought or confused, some gentle probing may be required to establish just what the grievance is. Your careful investigation of the who, what, when, where and why of the matter not only gets you the vital statistics but has a bracing effect on the other person. Not only does it suggest that action will be taken, but it gets him off the emotional level, and back into the realm of reason and facts. If the problem seems complex or technical in nature, you may wish to let the other person know that you're taking notes on it or reviewing file materials.

Step Four: Provide feedback. After you've completed your questioning, recite the story back to the caller for confirmation. This procedure allows misunderstandings to be corrected promptly, encourages elaboration on salient points and may jog the caller's memory about other aspects of the matter. It also lets him or her verify that you've listened attentively and thoroughly understand the problem.

Should you determine at this point that a clearcut mistake has been made, a gracious apology is much more effective in regaining goodwill than a plethora of excuses. It's disarming to hear an honest, "I was wrong" or "There's no excuse for this error, but I'll get immediately to work to put it right."

Step five: Describe the problem-solving procedure you'll use. Unless the complaint is simple enough to solve on the spot—say by promising an adjustment to the next bill or immediate shipment of missing merchandise—you should indicate what your plan for action is and when it can be accomplished. Avoid overly optimistic time estimates or tentative commitments that you might not be able to deliver on later.

It's often helpful to ask the other person how he or she'd like to have the problem resolved, rather than merely list options. Too much choice may add confusion or suggest time-consuming or complex solutions that the caller wouldn't dream of asking for on his or her own. This also directs the caller's attention in a positive direction—toward the solution—rather than retaining the focus on the problem itself.

SAYING "NO" DIPLOMATICALLY

While it's not too difficult to sell an unconditional "yes" to the caller's demands—though it may enhance your image to present the decision as a special favor or one that you've fought hard to achieve—a full or partial "no" needs delicate handling. Tactics to try include:

• **Stress fairness and facts, not personalities.** Some callers, once they realize that they're not going to get what they want, may make provocative remarks. It's important to avoid rising to the bait; instead, repeat the facts in a firm, pleasant way. Show the caller that you're convinced that the solution you offer is fair and reasonable and that once he's reflected on it further he'll come to see it the same way. You'll be surprised how often he'll end up apologizing for his attitude or backing down on his demands if you avoid any suggestion of a personal attack on him.

• **Give a reason for the turndown, and sound regretful.** It's especially infuriating when offering a complaint to run up against a blank wall like, "It's against company policy," or some other capricious-sounding refusal. Instead, you might say something like, "Given the seasonal nature of our merchandise, we feel that it would be unfair to us to accept returns more than thirty days after shipment as we would no longer be able to resell the goods. I'm sorry that you didn't see that notice printed in our catalog."

• **Emphasize whatever concessions you can make.** Even a small concession can help retain goodwill if you present it correctly: "While it's not possible to give a refund for speical orders, as I've explained, what I can do is give you the volume discount on your next order if it exceeds three-hundred units, rather than the normal four-hundred."

• **When appropriate, tell him how to appeal the decision.** You might refer him to a superior, suggest to whom he can protest in writing, or advise him of other procedures to secure a hearing of his grievance.

• **Finish on an "up" note by suggesting how the problem could be avoided in the future.** A complaint should be considered a request for information, which makes it a natural opportunity to present a low-key sales effort. Since the caller feels that you owe him or her something, you might offer to fill this need through a special sales effort, such as offering "inside" intelligence on future bargains or sales not generally advertised or revealing how to get additional discounts or other considerations.

You might also stress any procedures you could institute to keep the caller from hitting the same snag next time: "While an adjustment isn't possible for the reasons I've just described, what I can do is attach a flag to your account, so that our sales representative will make sure that your orders qualify for our bonus program."

CREATIVE COMPLAINING

The telephone can also be *your* hotline to action when you have a complaint of your own. Yet, according to a survey done by the U.S. Office of Consumer Affairs, 60 percent of those who are dissatisfied with an *expensive* purchase never bother to complain at all, most likely because they're convinced they won't get results. (The survey doesn't report how many of us let little grievances go by without a whimper of protest.)

With a touch of the finger, however, prompt resolution of their complaints—or yours—might be just a toll free call away. Currently over forty thousand companies in the U.S. maintain toll free 800 numbers for consumer use. (For information, call 800-555-1212; or order a directory of toll free consumer numbers from AT&T by calling 800-246-8686.)

Numbers for companies without a local listing or toll free number can often be found in *Standard and Poor's Register of Corporations, Directors and Executives*. In many areas, you can let your fingers do the walking by calling your librarian and having him or her look up the number in either this directory or the phone book for the right geographical area (many libraries stock current directories for most parts of the nation).

To make sure your complaint won't fall on deaf ears when you reach the company, prepare a brief summary of the problem and assemble receipts, account numbers and invoices before placing the call. Also decide precisely what you want—a replacement part, refund or redo of the job, for example. When you make the call, ask the person on the other end for his name and rank, and secure a commitment either to a course of action or a date when action can be taken.

Still no satisfaction? A free publication called *Consumer's Resource Handbook*, which will help you decide which government agency to call about your complaint, is available by writing to Consumer Information Center, Pueblo, CO 81009. You can also call the Better Business Bureau in your area— nationally there are 199 of them—to check the complaint record of any company you plan to do business with or to file a complaint.

A third place to call is the industry association of the firm your grievance is with; the Major Appliance Consumer Action Panel, for example, reports that it's resolved 80 percent of the complaints brought before it to the satisfaction of the consumer. The names and numbers of trade and other groups are listed in Gale Research's *Encyclopedia of Associations*.

DIALING FOR OVERDUE DOLLARS

Collecting tardy payments by telephone has several advantages over other methods. It's faster and cheaper than writing, harder to ignore and permits a personalized approach. Not only can you learn why the payment has been delayed—and act on any outstanding complaint or negotiate a payment plan—but you can secure a rapid commitment to action.

Good organization is the key to successful collection efforts. The sooner you contact the debtor, the greater the odds of shaking loose the payment—and the more psychological impact you'll have with your call. Secondly, scheduling your calls and follow-ups at precise intervals (say, every two weeks) has a cumulative effect of impressing the debtor with your unrelenting seriousness about getting the money. Finally, systematic escalation—starting with the gentlest of nudges and working up to intense, urgent appeals—creates a psychological climate that favors your eventual success, even with the more chronically slow.

Here's a five-step phone plan to speed those checks through the mail—and into your bank account.

1. Prepare a tactful opening. Since the delinquent payer is an established customer who may well be a good source of business in the future, a blend of firmness and tact is essential. After all, the other person might have a valid reason for nonpayment, such as an unresolved complaint or missing shipment. Or he may just have lost or forgotten about the bill. Acting on this assumption will create a tone of positive expectation, while a confrontational tone may actually strengthen the debtor's resolve not to pay by making him angry.

The best beginning is to introduce yourself and the company, then state the facts succinctly: "I'm calling about the September balance of three hundred dollars, which is now past due on your account." Then, pause for several seconds. This gentle jog avoids accusations, makes the purpose of the call apparent and may extract a promise of payment from the merely forgetful.

2. Use fact-finding questions to identify the payment problem. Let's assume that silence follows your initial statement or the customer makes some noncommittal response like, "Oh, is it?" To advance the conversation, you might inquire politely, "Did you receive this invoice?" or "Do you have any questions about the bill or the shipment?" This courteously confronts the customer with the existence of the debt and forces him to acknowledge it, but it allows him an opportunity to present his reasons or excuses for not paying (if any).

3. Pin down a payment plan. Once you've established the facts of any outstanding complaints or problems that may be holding up payment and have gained pertinent details of the debtor's current situation, you're ready to convert this information into a firm commitment. Ask your most crucial question now: "When may we expect to receive your payment?" Should the answer be a vague one like, "After we get the check from our distributor," "Soon" or "After the first of the month," follow up with a slightly more aggressive line of questioning: "When is the earliest that would be? Can you promise payment by September seventh? Well then, can I put you down for the ninth? How about the tenth?"

Having the debtor's account history in front of you will help you to negotiate effectively should you encounter resistance. You might appeal to his pride by citing his previous excellent payment record; to his sense of fairness by matter-of-factly reviewing your contractual arrangements with him; to his self-interest by showing how he could gain more advantageous terms in the future through prompt payment (such as discounts); or as a last resort, to fear by indicating the sterner measures to follow should he persist in his delinquency. What you want to *avoid* is a tone of begging or indicating you need the money personally.

4. *Answer objections.* If the other person voices objections to the arrangements you propose, your first tactic should be to establish exactly what the issue is. Often, the sole problem is the date of payment you've suggested, in which case you might try a bit of role reversal and say, "Well then, what do *you* propose?" If the reply is an extended payment plan or a definite promise of partial payment and a vaguer indication as to when the balance would be sent, the best tactic is to push for firmer arrangements and faster payments:

Debtor: I suppose I could send the eight hundred dollars from January early next month.

You: That would be on March first, then. Now will you also be sending the outstanding balance of $1,645 from February on that date?

Debtor: Well it depends on when I get in the money from the royalties I was telling you about.

You: Why don't we say that you'll send $1,225 on the first. That would retire half your debt, and you could send the balance ten days later, on the eleventh. How does that sound?

Debtor: I'll try.

You: Good. I'll mark down that we'll have $1,225 from you on the first, and $1,220 on the eleventh.

5. *Close on a courteous note.* A smooth wrap-up for the call is to confirm the plan, by repeating it one final time to impress it firmly upon the other person's mind, and to thank him or her for the promise of payment. Should the customer prove to have valid reasons for slow payment or continue to seem like a good credit risk, you might go one step further—with a sales message.

Once you have the account out—and the customer on the phone—you might point out that, judging by his previous buying patterns, he'll soon be needing additional goods or services from you. Or you might alert him to upcoming sales or specials, soon-to-be-released products, or other sales information, showing that you envision a continuing relationship with him and his company. With a diplomatic approach you could soon find yourself doubly rewarded for the call—with the past due payment in hand and a good order to add to your future profits!

PART THREE: PERFORMANCE

Getting the Most from Your Phone

12

EQUIPMENT: BEYOND BASIC BLACK

Were Alexander Bell making his historical phone call to his research assistant today, he'd have the option of lifting up his Liberace phone (made by Select Merchandise, Inc.) and watching a miniature of the entertainer pick up his tiny telephone and play the piano; of placing the call from his automobile, boat or plane; of sending exact copies of documents or visual material; of swapping computer data or of holding a video teleconference. With some systems, Bell could initiate the call simply by *glancing* at his telephone and saying aloud, "Call Watson!"

Of course, no matter which technology he employed, in the modern world the response to Bell's call might well have been Watson's voice, intoning, "At the sound of the beep, record your message." However, to reduce the time wasted on telephone tag, Bell might then try to call later with one-touch dialing; send a prerecorded message of his own via an unmanned auto-dialer; arrange contact through a "voice mail" service or system or send a brief message to Watson's alphanumerical pager.

BELLS AND WHISTLES

Wondering if it's time to update *your* business phones to put more power at your fingertips, raise the I.Q. of the office or trim costs?

Before you start selecting your phones, you may be curious about the economics of buying equipment versus renting it from the telephone company. While your cost of leasing business phones is tax deductible, the benefits of phone ownership are so overwhelming that over 70 million consumers have returned their leased equipment to the phone company since the 1984 break-up of the Bell System. Not only do you eliminate the fixed expense of leasing, but you may be eligible for an investment tax credit on your purchase price, and you may be able to depreciate the balance of the cost over the useful life of the equipment. (Your tax advisor or an IRS representative should be able to supply the applicable schedules and regulations.) The real bottom line on ownership, however, is that when you buy, it's an *asset*—not an endless drain on your cash flow.

Even if yours is among the 94 percent of U.S. businesses that use six or fewer lines—or among the 39 percent that get by with just *one* line—an increasingly sophisticated array of telephone features are now available to you. The basic black box that merely makes and receives calls is rapidly becoming obsolete, today, over 60 percent of the phones purchased include one or more "intelligent" features.

Here's a brief guide to making intelligent telephone choices for your business:

Feature Phones: Want a telephone that knows a trick or two—at a relatively affordable price? Unlike the conventional phones supplied for basic use by the phone company, these multifunction phones offer such conveniences as:

• **Speedy dialing.** Nimble-fingered callers need not wait for the clicks to stop before pressing the next number—instead the phone "remembers" what you've pressed and catches up. Most models allow you the option of using either pulse or tone dialing. This can save you money: since some areas charge extra for a touch-tone line, your pushbutton phone can emulate the dialing sounds of the old-fashioned rotary phone, while letting you enjoy the ease and speed of pushbutton calling. When making long distance calls or using tone-activated telephone services, you'd just switch to the tone-dialing mode.

• **Memory.** Let your phone enhance your memory by storing the numbers of the customers and associates you call frequently. You want to look at both how many separate numbers can be stored—some models can be programmed with up to one hundred entries—and how many digits are permitted in each entry. Some phones let you enter as many as thirty separate digits in each number—handy if your long distance service requires an elaborate dialing sequence—such as its phone number, your access code and the individual's own area codes and number—or for making overseas calls.

To make the most of this feature, you'll also want to buy a phone with a "Pause" button to insert delays into the dialing sequence. That way you'll provide time for the long distance carrier's computer to answer and receive the additional digits. (Further details on long distance carriers can be found in the next chapter.)

• **One-touch dialing.** After your phone is programmed with the numbers you call frequently—and any emergency numbers you want quick access to—some phones let you retrieve them with special dedicated keys. On other phones, you retrieve stored numbers by pressing the "Memory" key plus a one- or two-digit number used for that dialing sequence. Both kinds of phones provide a convenient index of the codes for stored numbers.

   • **Redial.** The phone's memory retains the digits of the last number you called, allowing you, at the touch of a finger, to retry your call should you encounter a busy signal. A further refinement of this feature, found on more expensive models, is auto-redial, which will continue trying the call until (depending on the model) you either get connected, place a different call or a specified time period passes. During the intervals between its calling attempts, the phone automatically hangs itself up to avoid blocking incoming calls.

   • **Save.** This feature allows you to hold any number for later redialing, even if you make other calls in between.

   • **Memory back-up.** After programming your dialing sequences into your phone, you'll want to avoid the annoyance of reentering this information should your phone be accidentally unplugged or encounter a power outage. Choosing a phone with battery back-up keeps you from losing this information during temporary electrical disturbances. You'll want to check how long the batteries keep the memory active—in one test of several popular models, the range varied from just five minutes to a full two hours.

   • **Mute button.** Hold this button down, and the other person can no longer hear you, while you retain the ability to listen to him. Convenient during negotiations if you want a quick, confidential consultation with an associate in the room. It's a discreet way to put the other person on hold—without his realizing it—while hearing everything he might say to *his* associates.

• **Digital display.** Some phones show the number dialed plus the date and time you placed the call. Helpful if you are maintaining a phone log.

• **Voice dialing.** A few more-expensive phones are now equipped with voice recognition devices that permit them to obey verbal orders, such as "Call George." The phone works by memorizing the sound of your voice reciting up to one hundred names, which it then associates with phone numbers of up to twenty-one digits that you enter manually. To make a call, you lift the receiver, utter the appropriate name and wait for the telephone to match it with the correct voice-print and then dial the number. A car model made by Innovative Devices, of Santa Clara, California, offers "no hands" calling—letting you concentrate on steering rather than calling.

• **Keyboard dialing.** A variation on this theme is the memory-equipped telephone, manufactured by Colonial Data Technologies, that places calls when the name of the desired individual is typed on its keyboard.

• **On/off ringer.** This option lets you turn off the bell on your extension when you don't wish to be disturbed—say, during an important meeting. A further point to keep in mind when selecting your phone is that many of the newer models don't ring as loudly as the more familiar standard phones—a problem for those with hearing difficulties. However, moderately priced bell ringers (which sound like the ring of a rotary phone) and louder outdoor ringers can be purchased at radio or phone supply stores as add-ons for most phones.

Speaker phones: A step up from the enhanced basic telephone, speaker phones have their pros and cons. Advantages include hands-free operation—allowing you to look over a report, take notes or do other tasks as you speak—and the possibility of holding a teleconference between the caller and associates who have gathered in your office. The major drawback is acoustical: Speaker phones are sometimes known as "squawk boxes" due to their characteristically hollow-sounding transmission. You may also find that your speaker phone tends to pick up extraneous noises, such as the shuffling of papers, further diminishing the quality of voice reproduction.

Should you feel that the conveniences outweigh this minus, you have two choices. You can buy a new telephone, either corded or cordless, with built-in speakers, or save money by equipping your existing telephone with a speaker adapter. These typically have modular cords that just plug into your current phone jack.

Cordless phones: Like to stroll around your office while you chat or bring your phone with you when you confer with others in the building? Cordless phones range from inexpensive, no-frills versions to deluxe, memory-equipped models. While the options may vary, the phones themselves are composed of two parts: a base that plugs both into an electrical outlet and a telephone jack; and a handset or receiver that sends and receives signals from the base. When not in use, the handset is placed on the base for recharging of its batteries.

Features to look for include:

• **Sound quality.** One problem that buyers encounter with these phones is the difficulty of judging the sound quality of the phone effectively in the store. Store owners report that in some areas, customers complain of electrical interference from nearby radio stations or railroad tracks—which is why you should investigate refund policies before making the investment. Some models have scanners that search through ten different calling frequencies to locate the clearest channel for your call or allow you to switch channels to bypass interference.

• **Range.** Most models can send and receive signals from between seven hundred and fifteen hundred feet of the base. Experts say the models with the fifteen hundred range generally have superior sound quality at all distances from the base— making them the better buy.

• **Security codes.** The most up-to-date models feature as many as three hundred different, personalized security codes. The reason is that an uncoded phone is vulnerable to unauthorized use—it's possible for someone with a cordless receiver of their own to drive through the neighborhood and place long distance calls on your line without your knowledge. Security codes prevent this potentially costly form of telephone theft.

• **Base phone:** A few cordless phones offer a complete phone both at the base and on the cordless receiver. While you speak on the receiver, a second person can use the built-in speaker phone at the base for hands-free participation in the call. An intercom also lets you conduct such maneuvers as answering the call at the base, paging a second person at the handset and transferring the call.

• **User-friendly batteries.** After you've used your cordless phone a few years, the rechargeable batteries will usually require replacement. By selecting a model that lets the consumer make the change—rather than the manufacturer— you'll avoid downtime while your phone is being serviced, and save the cost of labor as well. Some cordless phones have dual battery packs—one is always being charged while the other is in use.

Cellular phones: First introduced in 1983, the cellular mobile phone has become the hottest innovation in telephone technology in recent years. Over the past two years sales have risen 800 percent, and the Cellular Telecommunications Industry Association predicts that by 1990 over three million of them will be in use in the U.S. As sales go up, the prices are actually going *down*: The average price of a portable mobile phone is 20 percent lower today than in 1985, while the price of a car phone has declined by 40 percent. Experts anticipate even more dramatic price cuts over the next five years—projecting that the cost of equipment may be only one-third of today's prices and the cost of service comparable to home phone rates.

The business applications are almost endless; a recent New York *Times* story described a real estate agent who uses her car phone to speed the showing of houses on her list; a stockbroker who combines business and pleasure by staying in the thick of the financial action from his box at the baseball stadium; a taco cart owner who receives advance orders by phone to reduce the lines at lunchtime; even a drug dealer who eludes call tracing as he makes shady deals for his illegal wares.

As calls can be made or taken from almost anywhere, you'll find that cellular phones can expand your business presence: When key employees are on the move—between appointments, say—you can reach them for instant information to capture a sale or conduct more effective negotiations; and when it's you that's in transit, decision-making authority is readily accessible to those working below you. Or should you find yourself delayed in reaching that important customer, a quick call from you defuses annoyance. Travel time can become a productive—and potentially profitable—portion of your workday, rather than a loss of time or money.

Since cellular phones work as radio transmissions between "cells," or areas of two to ten miles in size, their drawback is that the signals can be intercepted and monitored by anyone with the right equipment—a consideration if you're conducting delicate negotiations or other confidential business. Although monitoring cellular conversations has been ruled illegal under wire-tapping statutes, it's said to be relatively simple to do—and a popular pastime for some.

Service is currently available in over three hundred regions, mostly centered in major cities, but is expected to encompass more rural areas in the near future. U.S. companies have also penetrated such overseas markets as Britain and Hong Kong.

Some shopping considerations to keep in mind:

• **Anticipated use.** Since portable cellular telephones are priced roughly 60 percent higher than car phones, on average, your first decision is whether the premium price of the portable is a cost-effective decision for you. Should you plan to set up a network of the phones for yourself and your staff, you'll also want to investigate whether quantity discounts can be negotiated with the vendor you've selected, on both the equipment and the monthly service fees.

• **Features desired.** The more frills you select, the higher the price. Among the available features are: hands-free operation, built-in message recorder, electronic lock, data voice connection (allows transmission of computer data), electronic scratch pad memory (lets you store a new number in memory while you are in the middle of a conversation), built-in speaker phone, last number recall, on-hook dialing (no need to lift the receiver to place a call), call timer, dial number display and storage of up to one hundred numbers in memory.

• **Installation.** Since proper installation is essential to the optimal operation of the system, you'll want to shop around for the best price and workmanship. If you're purchasing a new car you may also wish to investigate installation by your car dealer. With leased cars—or those you expect to trade in soon— you'll want to check the price and practicality of transferring the phone to your next automobile.

• **Reputation of the manufacturer.** Currently there are about forty-five operators of cellular phone services in the U.S., but market analysts believe that it's unlikely that all will survive in the increasingly competitive marketplace. Since you don't want to find yourself orphaned when you need service or repairs, choosing one of the larger, more established companies might be the best bet even if prices are slightly higher. In addition to the seven Bell "wireline" companies offering cellular phones, the giants right now are McCaw Cellular, LIN Broadcasting, Metro Mobile CTS, Metromedia, Cellular Communications, and Mobile Communication Corp.

Multiline phones: If yours is one of the 61 percent of businesses requiring multiple telephone lines, there are three ways to obtain multiline capacity. The least expensive, lowest tech option is the old fashioned *electromechanical telephone*, which normally can handle up to twenty-nine lines and a hold button. You can recognize this type of phone by its rather thick cable. The main advantage of an electromechanical telephone, other than low cost, is, in the words of one phone consultant, that it's "almost bulletproof"; the main drawback is the high expense of installation and lack of the more sophisticated features of other systems.

The most popular type of multiline phone, however, is the *square key system*. Pete Caminiti, the president of Westchester Business Phone, Inc., reports that among his customer base, "eight-five percent are good prospects for this type of system." Such systems, which can currently accommodate as many as thirty lines and one hundred phones (and capacity is being upgraded steadily), are composed of electronic feature phones, each of which is identical to its brethren in the system.

Among the useful features you can expect to find in this type of system are:

• **Toll restriction.** To reduce unauthorized or personal use of your business phones for long distance calling by employees, you can allow or deny access to certain area codes. Each employee's access can be custom-tailored—allowing executives to make calls without restriction, while confining low-level staffers to calls to nearby areas, say.

• **Cost-accounting.** This lets you monitor who's calling where, helping you to detect telephone abuse or allocate toll charges among different departments.

• **Unattended conferencing.** This feature allows an associate at the office to connect an important call to you when you're on the road or at another location, then drop out of the call. Callers need not even know that you're not at your desk. Since it's an unattended conference, the person who connected you is no longer party to the call—preserving privacy and freeing him or her for other business or calling.

There's also an interesting conference feature on some low-cost two-line telephones currently available. By using a "call merge" feature, you can make or receive a call on one line, put the caller on hold and interconnect it with a call you've made or received on the other line, permitting a three-way conversation.

• **Automatic call diversion.** Evening and weekend calls—or those received when the office is empty—can be transferred to

another number, such as your home, or to an answering
service.

• **Dual-color LEDs.** Which of those twelve flashing lines is
your incoming call? Choose a system that shows one color for
calls in progress, another for new incoming calls, suggests Pete
Caminiti, and you'll avoid confusing yourself and your callers.

• **Calling displays.** On some telephones you can see at a
glance such information as how long you've been speaking on
the current call, verification of the number you've just dialed
(avoid wasting time or money on wrong numbers), what calls
are waiting and what other system users have left messges for
you in your absence. You can also leave a message of your own,
for your delegate, for example, that your call should be transferred to another office.

• **Dedicated private line.** You can program the system to
provide a private line for yourself. However, since all the phones
are the same, that particular key position will then be unusable
on all the other phones in the system.

The third type of multiline system is the PBX, or private
branch exchange, which is normally the most expensive option
but has the largest capacity. Such systems can be configured
in a variety of ways, the most typical being as a stand-alone
PBX, where incoming calls are handled by a console attendant
who greets the caller and connects him with the desired
extension. The system can also be configured as a key phone
system, supporting feature phones, or as part of a larger PBX
(in a small site adjoining the corporate headquarters, for example).

Answering machines: Though Code-A-Phone introduced a
primitive version of the telephone answering machine back in

1958, the true boom times for the "beep" only arrived in the 1980s. 1986 sales of almost five million units represent a 400 percent increase over 1982 levels—while the average price of a basic machine has dropped by 40 percent during the same time period. This surge in popularity—one phone customer in ten now has a machine—has created a growing acceptance of the device: One 1985 survey showed that 70 percent of us are willing to put our words on tape, while one industry analyst found more recently that "Now people are annoyed when they *can't* leave a message."

Here are some features to look for:

• **Greeting length**. A fixed-length greeting—say, of twenty seconds—limits your creativity in composing the outgoing message, as your words might either be clipped off at the end, or be followed by dead air before the beep. A variable length greeting—that lets you speak for anywhere between a few seconds to several minutes—is far more convenient.

• **Remote control**. Surveys indicate that the most popular feature is the ability to call your machine from a distant phone and hear your messages. What you do is signal the machine with the sounds of certain touch-tone keys or a beeper provided with the machine and then listen to the playback of any messages recorded during your absence.

Each system of remote playback has its pros and cons. With the beeper, there's the potential problem of forgetting or losing it, and the hassle of having an extra piece of equipment to lug around (it's about the size of a pocket calculator). In the other system, there's the necessity of finding a touch-tone phone to use while calling in for messages, since the machine won't respond to the sounds of a rotary phone.

• **Remote monitoring**. Some answering machines and speaker phones allow you to telephone from an outside phone and briefly listen in on the sounds in the room where the phone is located.

• **Security**. If you're concerned by the possibility of others' eavesdropping on your business messages, you'll want to consider how secure the remote system is. Beepers that emit a series of tones—rather than those that signal with a single tone—increase security by making the "code" more difficult to crack. The units that use touch tones to activate remote playback are most secure when the manufacturer allows you to select your own three-digit code—instead of programming in its own—and lets you change the code at will.

• **Toll-saver**. You'll avoid unnecessary long distance charges if you buy a machine with this ringing feature. It works this way: your telephone will answer on the first or second ring when any messages have been recorded, on the fourth if none have been. At the third ring, you'd just hang up, knowing that no message was waiting.

• **Time and date**. Some models have a synthesized voice that announces the time and/or date when the call was received at the end of the message—handy if you're wondering whether the call came in before or after the last time you spoke with that person.

• **Call-forwarding**. Want to learn of your messages the moment they come in? Some machines can be programmed to call you at any number you leave (or one that you transmit remotely after you've arrived) and beep you. You then enter the correct code and hear the message.

• **Announce only**. Many answering machines allow the option of only broadcasting an outgoing message without recording incoming messages—helpful when you want callers to try you at another number or time, or when you want to publicize an upcoming event or sale or inform others of the new location or date of a conference you're holding.

• **Other recording uses.** Some answering machines can be used to tape telephone conservations you hold, to leave recorded memos to other office personnel or to take your dictation.

• **Hybrid machines.** Want to save desk space—and possibly money? Another option is to buy one of the new self-answering telephones. There are several models available that combine a telephone and answering machine in a single unit. You'll want to evaluate your selection carefully in terms of both uses: Some units work significantly better in one mode than the other or don't include as wide an array—or as many combinations—of features as separate machines might.

Pagers: Pagers are now half the size and price they were just one year ago, according to industry experts, and not surprisingly paging services are reporting a brisk demand: Currently there are five million business and consumer subscribers in the U.S. The models available come in sizes as small as a fountain pen, are available in a wide spectrum of colors and signal silently to the user with flashing lights or a gentle tingling motion.

Among the new services being offered are:

• **Alphanumerical papers.** These display both letters and numbers, letting the wearer know who is calling him or her or to receive a basic typed message on a small screen on the pager. Your callers can, in effect, send a brief letter to you—with the speed of a phone call. Some alphanumerical pagers can hold as many as ten different messages or telephone numbers; others can be plugged into a printer to deliver a hard copy of the communication.

• **Voice mail.** Callers using a touch-tone phone can leave their message on your answering machine, which will then alert you that a message is waiting by paging you.

• **Special services.** By linking your pager into the cellular frequencies used by your car or mobile phone, you can arrange to be alerted should calls come into one of those phones during your absence. Or by linking the fire or burglar alarm at your home, office or warehouse to a telephone, your pager could be used as a first warning system to notify you of burglars or a fire.

• **National or regional paging.** A soon-to-be available service, according to industry insiders, is a network of paging services that would allow subscribers to be paged anywhere in the country. Other projects under development include various custom paging services, such as being paged and reminded of one's upcoming appointments during the day; obtaining stock quotes or sports scores; or being alerted to other timely events, such as a rapid price move in a stock you were following.

Fascimile transmission: "Fax" machines, which can transmit one or more pages of words or images over telephone lines, have finally reached the mass market. Their high speed—a printed page can be sent around the world in forty seconds—and increasingly low prices are making them more and more attractive to small-business owners, home-office workers, and general consumers: Experts say that these groups may make up 50 percent of the market by 1990.

Using a fax machine might be compared to inserting

material—such as graphics, text or photographs—into a photocopier at one end of the line and having a copy (of varying quality, depending on the machines used) appear on the other end. Among the possible uses are: the ability to make instant credit checks on customers; to send a completely accurate copy of an important order, contract or specification almost instantaneously to any of the millions of fax users in the world; to arrange transmissions at off hours to cut long distance costs or reach geographically distant associates during *their* normal business hours and to send text with foreign language characters without needing a special keyboard with which to receive or transmit it.

There's a wide range of models from which to select. The more elaborate—and expensive—faxes offer features like the capacity to store dozens of phone numbers and hundreds of pages; to auto-dial stored numbers to send outgoing messages at any time of day or night you've specified, or to automatically take incoming fax calls and receive transmissions; to send a single document automatically to several locations, or to send different documents to a list of individuals you've specified; to crisply reproduce signatures, photos and graphics; to send material to computers; and to scan an oversized original, such as a computer spreadsheet, and transmit it for receipt in a smaller format.

At much lower cost there are the new "personal" faxes, which combine the functions of fax, telephone, answering machine and copier. There's also a portable fax too which transmits on battery power from a plane, train, car or any other location with a telephone. Or your personal computer can double as fax machine when enhanced by a fax circuit board and optical charcter reader. To support half-tones (used on photographs) or elaborate graphics, your computer may need additional circuit boards. Your overall reproduction quality will also depend on the printer you're using with the system.

A new directory, *The Original Fax Phone Book,* lists the fax numbers in the U.S., Canada, Mexico and Puerto Rico. There's also an international section with entries from all foreign countries: Australia through the United Kingdom. The twelve-hundred-page book has sections on such topics as how to obtain international fax phone numbers not in the book, tips on getting more out of your fax machine and a variety of other topics. (To order or get more information, contact D.A.F. Information Systems, Inc., 230 College Street, Burlington, VT 05401.)

Modems: To use your computer or fax machine, you need a modem (*mo*dulater/*dem*odulater) to translate the machine's digital signals into analog signals that can be carried across phone lines. A modem on the other end then converts the signals back into a format usable by the other machine.

While there are a wide variety of modems on the market, most experts agree that the best choice is either a Hayes or a Hayes-compatible, 1,200-bits-per-second, stand-alone modem. ("Stand-alone" means that the modem is a separate unit, rather than being part of your computer or fax.)

The reason to choose a Hayes or Hayes-compatible modem is that Hayes is the major manufacturer of personal computer modems and has established the standards of quality and command language for today's micro modems. You will find that most communications software is designed to work with a Hayes or Hayes-compatible modem (these are modems made by other vendors that use the same command language).

The speed at which the modem operates is measured in bits per second (bps). Although there are modems that work at other speeds than 1,200 bps, the 300-bps modems are likely to seem uncomfortably slow—and will increase your telephone and computer time costs. The newer 2,400-bps modems, on the other hand, are not available from all vendors and may not be cost-effective for many users.

A recent innovation is the cellular modem, sold by cellular phone vendors, which transmits data from a laptop computer. With these devices and your car or mobile phone, you can maintain your competitive edge by turning a remote workplace or your car into a mobile office—at the touch of a finger.

COMMUNICATION CONSULTANTS

Need some expert assistance in selecting the right telephone technology for your business? If you're planning a substantial investment in equipment or have highly complex needs, you may want to hire a communications consultant (consult the yellow pages for listings of consultants in your area) to analyze your phone needs, help you choose appropriate equipment and services, and supervise installation. Some consultants will also perform any needed service or maintenance and will arrange to have your equipment moved or upgraded as necessary.

In selecting consultants or vendors, Pete Caminiti points out that the objective isn't just to get up and running initially, but to establish a continuing relationship. "Many people go about it the wrong way: They give themselves a crash course in what's out there by contacting a few vendors, and buy the phones that sound closest to their needs. What they should be doing is thinking *ahead*—about things like the overall reputation of the vendor and the quality of service available—and looking for a vendor who'll keep them technically competitive both now and in the future."

13

CHEAPER TALK

Today's high tech telephone services let you do far more than just "reach out and touch someone," as a recently reported case illustrates. When a Pennsylvania department store manager had his evening disrupted by an obscene caller, revenge was just a couple of keystrokes away. By pressing "*69" on his telephone, he prompted an automatic return of the call. Seconds later, the manager had the unsuspecting perpetrator on the line, and shouted, "You just called my house, and I don't appreciate what you said!" After mumbling an apology, the stunned prankster asked, "How did you know it was me?" "Easy," replied the manager. "My telephone is smarter than you are."

Another telephone, located at Bally's Casino Hotel in Atlantic City, may have outsmarted the Grim Reaper. Programmed into this hotel's internal phone system was a new service—know as Identa Call—which displays a caller's phone number on a small screen by the phone. When a desperate heart attack victim called the front desk for aid, but collapsed without giving a name or room number, casino employees were able to locate the caller immediately and provide prompt aid.

Are your dialing dollars buying you *the* smartest, most cost-effective service? If you haven't reviewed your calling needs—and the new services available to help you meet them efficiently—during the last six to twelve months, you may be missing out on opportunities to increase profits or trim costs by altering your purchasing decisions. This chapter's smart money guide to the telephone services marketplace will acquaint you with some of your options, but bear in mind that some newer services haven't yet penetrated to all calling areas. Consult local and long distance carriers for full details, prices and brochures before ordering.

LOCAL OPTIONS

Your local carrier may offer some or all of these services:

• **Call-forwarding.** Hate to miss an important call or let your customers and associates feel out of touch? With this service, you can "program" your telephone so your calls will be transferred to wherever you might be—or to a delegate you've selected, such as an assistant or answering service or machine. However, you will be charged for the cost of having the calls forwarded.

• **Remote call-forwarding.** You can establish a local identity for your business in any area or area code within your state with this service—without the expense of setting up branch offices. You are assigned a local number in each area you select—and listed in white- and yellow-page directories for that area. Customers then call the local number, at economically attractive local rates, and their calls will be automatically transferred to your main number (you pay all direct-dial costs for each call).

• **Call waiting.** Your single-line telephone can do double duty with this service. Should a second call come in when you're already on the line, rather than receive an annoying busy signal, the caller can still reach you. You hear a clicking sound and can put the first caller on hold and answer the second call.

• **Three-way calling.** Set up your own three-way conference calls or consultations—with the same ease as placing an ordinary call.

• **Speed calling.** This lets a conventional telephone emulate a memory dialer. You can arrange to have your local carrier store either eight or thirty numbers in its computers, which are then associated with a couple of digits on your telephone. The service works with both tone- and pulse-dialing telephones. One point to consider, however, is that buying a memory telephone may well be a better investment than endless paying monthly costs for this service.

• **Intrastate 800 service.** Marketing experts maintain that by using a tollfree 800 number in your ads, you can increase your sales by 20 percent or more. Customers outside of your immediate area are more motivated to place a long distance call at your expense than their own; and an 800 number can also be useful in handling customer questions on billing, service or complaints. Since 800 service is priced according to how large an area you opt to have covered, if most of your customers are intrastate, you'll save by limiting 800 service to that area.

• **Intrastate WATS.** Wide Area Telecommunications Service, or WATS, is available from local phone companies as well as AT&T. Intrastate service could offer substantial savings if your firm makes a high volume of toll calls within the state. Since there are fixed monthly access charges (as well as fees for individual calls), you'll want to review some of your typical phone bills with your telephone company service representative to determine whether potential savings justify the service.

• **Discount packages.** If your business is located in an area using "local measured service," where a separate fee is charged for each local call (as opposed to a flat rate for unlimited use), you may be able to slash your local costs by buying monthly blocks of calling time in areas that you telephone frequently. You'd pay a discounted rate for the time—only a savings, of course, if you actually use it all—and get further discounts on additional time beyond the minimum. Should you opt for this service, it pays to scrutinize your calling patterns at regular intervals to determine where block purchases might most effectively cut costs—and to add or subtract service in the appropriate areas.

• **Educational seminars.** Some local phone companies offer half- and full-day seminars on using the telephone more effectively in business. Two currently available programs are: "Telemarketing Skills," which emphasizes practical training in telephone sales, and "Telephone Techniques," which trains you in projecting the right company image to callers.

• **CLASS.** Several million telephone customers can currently enhance their phones' capabilities by subscribing to an array of services collectively referred to as Custom Local Area Signalling Services (CLASS), which use new communications software developed by AT&T and others.

One of the more popular CLASS options is *call-blocking*. By punching a single code into the telephone, the customer programs the phone to reject calls from certain local numbers. Jokes one sales representative, "I sometimes refer to this as our mother-in-law service." This service can be used with *distinc-*

tive ringing, a second CLASS option, to trill calls from certain local numbers with a special tone. You could use the two to block calls from overpersistent salespeople, while responding instantly to your genuinely important customers.

A third feature, *Identa Call,* lets display-equipped telephones show the number of the caller—handy if you're disconnected during the call or just wondering to whom that familiar-sounding voice belongs. *Call tracing* lets your telephone initiate a trace of an incoming local call by directing telephone company computers to scan an electronic directory of listings to determine the source of a call. Pranksters watch out!

• **Centrex.** Would you like the convenient features of a square-key or PBX system without having to purchase expensive new phones, or locking yourself into a system you might outgrow should your business expand rapidly? Centrex is a package of special features you pay your local phone company a monthly fee to use. Since the features are located in the lines, not within your telephone sets, your current equipment need not be upgraded or changed. Instead, the phone company provides the service from its premises—saving you office space as well as money.

Typical features include: direct inward and outward dialing (calls can be made and received without an attendant), intercom dialing (reach others within the organization by touching a few digits on the phone), centralized answering (select one of your telephones, say, the receptionist's, to serve as the answering center for your main number), do-it-yourself conference calling, line hunting (calls to busy numbers in the system are routed automatically to another preselected number), and a variety of call-forwarding and transferring options.

• **Vanity numbers.** Although special numbers like 1-800-USA ARMY have long been available for 800 subscribers, they're now also available to local residents and businesses through their phone company at modest monthly fees. The configuration of letters or numbers you select must be, say phone officials, "available, unique and not obscene." One disappointing note: Directory assistance and the white pages will list the number in numerical form; the yellow pages lets you advertise your number in the form you've selected.

• **Yellow pages advertising.** The first telephone directory was printed in 1878, two years after Alexander Bell's invention of the telephone. It consisted of a single page listing fifty names but no numbers. So few people had telephones that any of them could be reached merely by telling the operator the name of the party desired. While the first "yellow page" directory of classified business advertising followed in 1906, the business of printing directories has experienced its biggest boom in the years since the 1984 break-up of AT&T—over 175 new directories of business listings have appeared since then.

As a result, many advertisers find themselves puzzled as to how to spend their directory ad dollars. According to Statistical Research, a marketing-research firm, yellow-page directories are consulted by consumers over 45 million times a day— or 16 billion times a year. About 18 percent of all adults thumb through them in a typical day, and nearly half of those who look end up making a purchase within forty-eight hours. But in areas with competing books, advertisers face the choice of investing in smaller ads in all directories or a larger showing in one of them. Experts are saying that pressure from bewildered advertisers will force the directory publishers to audit their circulations, as do other media. Until then, most businesses are opting for the shotgun approach.

• **The talking phone book.** An innovative approach to telephone advertising has recently been developed by Infoplus of

Needham, Massachusetts. Yellow-page advertisers in New England and Arizona can arrange to also be included in a "Talking Phonebook." A four-digit code, provided in their ad, allows consumers to dial the central Infoplus number, punch in the code on their touch-tone phone and hear a recorded message supplied by the advertiser on such topics as store hours or the company's latest promotions or sales.

• **Avoiding junk calls.** Tired of lifting your receiver only to hear a computerized or unsolicited sales pitch of some sort? A new service will arrange to have your name removed—free of charge—from the telephone solicitation lists of many organizations. You can also arrange, through the same organization, to have your name deleted from commercial mailing lists— drastically reducing the number of junk letters and calls you receive. To stop unwanted calls, contact the Telephone Preference Service; for unwanted mail, the Mail Preference Service; both are part of the Direct Marketing Association, 6 East 43rd Street, New York, NY 10017, telephone 212-689-4977. The deletion of your name remains in effect for five years.

• **Putting social calls on hold.** Soon after installing software that tracked employee telephone calls, a Los Angeles insurance company discovered a mysterious pattern. Each day at precisely noon, someone in the company dialed a number in a neighboring community and stayed on the line fifty-eight minutes. Eventually the culprit was identified: A file clerk on that extension had her mother turn on the clerk's favorite soap opera and leave the telephone next to the TV. While such flagrant abuse of phone privileges may sound uncommon, a government survey found that a staggering twenty-nine percent to fifty percent of long distance calls placed by federal agency employees were personal calls.

Call-accounting hardware and software sales have risen almost 1,000 percent in the past seven years—and are now used in over sixty-three thousand firms. A monitoring system will typically result in a 20 percent to 60 percent drop in a company's phone bills during the first month of operation, say industry experts. In addition to checking up on employees, the system may also provide such services as routing long distance calls to the least expensive carrier, tracking telephone expenses incurred on behalf of each client and a variety of other tasks.

Although systems can cost from three thousand dollars for a system that handles up to sixty office extensions all the way up to eighty thousand dollars for a system with all the bells and whistles to handle five hundred extensions, there's a modest version, the CPA-1000, available at Radio Shack for less than one hundred dollars, that will keep track of both local and long distance calls made or received on a particular phone. Not only could you use it to reduce employee misuse of the phone, but it serves as a handy check of your phone company charges. Long distance companies have acknowledged that, on occasion, customers have been billed twice for the same call or for calls placed but not answered. The device could help protect against such errors.

• **Shared tenant services.** Thousands of businesses now have the option of locating themselves in a "smart" building, where tenants share expensive, centrally installed telecommunications equipment that provides crystal-clear voice and high speed data transmission, least-cost long distance routing, message forwarding, electronic mail, and teleconferencing. Basically, the building functions as a large PBX, offering state-of-the-art equipment and services at a fraction of the cost of buying and installing such services on your own. The business is expected to generate a sales volume of $380 million by 1990, according to industry analysts.

The potential points of concern are information security, the compatibility of the building's system with your existing phone equipment and the competence of the service personnel associated with the building. Larger companies may also find that dropping PBX prices make ownership the more economically attractive option for them.

LONG DISTANCE DECISIONS

The same group of nine representative calls could cost you between $18.60 and $20.95, according to a *Consumer Reports* test, depending on which long distance carrier they were routed through. The 8 percent price differential illustrates the current state of the long distance marketplace—though toll call savings are out there, the price wars of a few years ago, when some of AT&T's competitors were undercutting Ma Bell's costs by as much as 40 percent, are over. New telephone rules force competing carriers to pay the same rates as AT&T for local network connections in equal access areas (now about 70 percent of the U.S.), rather than the 55 percent discount they had enjoyed previously.

The result has been a market shakeout in the $50 billion long distance business. Even AT&T, which has retained 80 percent of the long distance business, has had to slash consumer prices by 10 percent while spending over $2 billion to upgrade its networks. The resulting squeeze on its larger competitors has prompted several mergers, while some smaller players are likely to simply drop out of the field in the future. As a consumer, you'll find that the various carriers are becoming more similar in their prices, transmission quality, and dialing convenience—meaning that you'll have to be a shrewder shopper to locate and capitalize on the bargains that are still available. Here's a look at tactics and current services:

• **Comparing costs.** If you are in an equal-access area, you must designate one long distance company as your primary carrier. If you don't, your local telephone company will randomly assign one to you. To determine which carrier is cheapest for your personal calling pattern, you either study previous bills to identify the areas you call most frequently and contact the various carriers to compare their rates to those cities; or you can arrange to have the calculations made for you by Consumer's Checkbook, a nonprofit research organization located in Washington, D.C.

Using their computer database of the rates of about fifty long distance carriers, Consumer's Checkbook will recalculate one of your typical telephone bills to show you exactly how much these same calls would have cost you with each of the carriers operating in your area. The cost of the service ranges from about ten dollars to seventy-five dollars, depending on the dollar volume of calls listed on the bill. For further information about the evaluation service, call toll free 800-441-8933.

• **Volume discounts.** If you customarily spend over twenty dollars a month on your toll calls, you'll probably qualify for some sort of volume discount with many carriers. You'll want to determine whether the discount applies to the entire bill should it exceed the required volume or only to the portion above some minimum cost. Another point to evaluate is whether the volume discount applies to calls made during the entire twenty-four hour period, or only at certain times. If the latter, you'll also want to check whether the specified time period is one during which you place enough calls to qualify.

To get volume discounts, you must either select that company as your primary carrier or establish a separate account with it. You'd then make the calls the same way as you'd have done before equal access went into effect: by dialing the second carrier's local number, entering your authorization code and then dialing the long distance number you want—a potentially time-consuming procedure should you lack a memory phone to assist you.

• **AT&T Pro America I, II and III.** While the volume discounts offered by alternate carriers are available to both business and residential customers, only business subscribers are eligible for three AT&T discount plans. These apply to interstate direct-dial calls using AT&T long distance service or AT&T card service for either voice, data or fascimile transmission. Calls that don't cross state boundaries, or are collect, person-to-person, or third party billing don't qualify.

AT&T Pro America I is designed for those businesses whose phone bills average at least $125 a month, but less than $500. Currently, for a $12.75 monthly fee, you'll get a 10 percent discount on direct-dialed out-of-state calls and a 5 percent discount on interstate card calls. There's also a one-time ten-dollar start-up fee.

AT&T Pro America II is for the customer with bills in the montly range of five hundred dollars to three thousand dollars, and it has an eighty-five-dollar-a-month fee. The calls are billed individually (unlike WATS service), in six-second increments, at rates based on distance, time of day and duration. AT&T Pro America III is for those spending two hundred to one thousand hours a month—or over three thousand dollars—on out-of-state calls. AT&T Pro service may also be available for calls made intrastate. For further information about any Pro service, call 800-222-0400.

• **Opportunity Calling.** Another, somewhat less appealing, AT&T program, available to business or residential customers, is its "Opportunity Calling." Each month that you spend over fifteen dollars on long distance calls, you "earn" one dollar for each dollar you've spent, to be applied as discounts on selected merchandise offered by companies participating in the program. However, you are limited as to the amount of your earned credits you can apply to the same purchase: You might be able, for example, to knock ten dollars off the price of a sixty dollar item.

• **Sign-up bonuses.** The alternate long distance carriers have special promotions from time to time where you can get, say, sixty minutes of free calling time or extra discounts on the first couple of bills. Since you can switch your primary carrier for free during the first six months after you've signed up and for a five-dollar fee after that, it might pay to switch should a particularly good bargain come along.

• **Gypsy dialing.** A money-saving feature of equal access that you might not be aware of is the possibility of using carriers other than your primary one simply by dialing a five-digit code. This feature, variously known as gypsy dialing, casual calling or code dialing, lets you shop around for the cheapest rate every time you place a long distance call. If you'd chosen AT&T as your carrier, for example, you'd pay $1.46 for a ten-minute late-night call from Albuquerque to Phoenix. But if you'd entered the five-digit code for U.S. Sprint, you'd pay $1.33. On the other hand, should you have required long distance directory assistance, it would cost you sixty cents to make the request of AT&T, and fifty-four cents from Allnet.

Calls you make through an alternate carrier are usually billed through your local telephone company. Some smaller carriers may require you to establish an account. You also will be ineligible for volume discounts when placing calls in this manner. A more detailed summary of code dialing rules can be obtained by calling each carrier you wish to use, or through the Telecommunications Research and Action Center, in Washington, D.C., (phone number 202-462-2520) which publishes a document named the "Long Distance Comparison Chart."

The following table contains the telephone numbers and codes for several major long distance carriers. To use gypsy dialing you'd prefix a long distance call by dialing the access code listed on the right hand side of the table. Also included are the toll free numbers of each company, for further information.

Carrier	Tollfree number	Access code
AT&T	800-222-0300	10288
MCI	listed locally	10222
Allnet	800-982-8888	10444
U.S. Sprint	800-531-4646	10777
Western Union	800-562-0240	10220
ITT	800-526-3000	10488

• **WATS.** Should your company spend more than fifteen hours a month making out-of-state toll calls, long distance WATS service might be an option to investigate. The basic out-of-state service calling area consists of the states immediately adjacent to your home state, while additional service areas enlarge upon this by widening the inclusive area. The largest service area covers the entire continental U.S., Alaska, Hawaii, Puerto Rico, and the U.S. Virgin Islands.

Contrary to the popular misconception about WATS service, the fee is *not* a flat rate for unlimited monthly calling (you might want to make sure employees understand this), but a one-time installation fee, a monthly charge for each WATS line and a per-call billing, which is calculated according to "taper points." The first fifteen hours of calling are charged at regular AT&T business day or evening rates; the first level of discounts covers 15.1 to 40 hours of monthly usage; and the heaviest discounts come with all usage over 40 hours. Late-night and weekend calls cost up to 56 percent off the business day price.

• **Dedicated private lines.** Does your company have one or more out-of-town branches that you contact frequently? If so, you may want to link them through a dedicated private line. Terminology varies according to the telephone systems used by your branches: Between two PBX systems, your link would be referred to as a *tie-line;* between a key and a PBX system, as an *off-premise extension;* and between two key systems as a *private line.*

Whatever the wording, however, the operating principle is the same: You can reach the other branch internally, without placing an outgoing call. Ringing on the other line would either be initiated just by picking up the receiver or by entering a few digits as an extension code. Your cost would be a flat monthly charge covering unlimited usage, meaning that the more you call, the better a bargain you'll be getting. Installation charges, alas, have skyrocketed since the AT&T break-up: In the past five years they've risen from under two hundred to twelve hundred dollars or higher.

• **FX lines.** Foreign exchange, or FX lines, link your office to a local exchange in another area. Outgoing calls you make to that area are billed as local calls (plus you pay a flat monthly rate for unlimited usage of your FX line), while callers from that area can reach you also by paying local rates. Not only does this let you establish a local presence in another area, as does remote call-forwarding, but it could cut your telephoning costs to an area where you do a very heavy volume of business.

• **Least-cost routing.** How would you like to have your *telephone* automatically route each long distance call you place to the least expensive carrier? This service is available with Centrex, and on many square-key or PBX systems. You'll enjoy the savings without the hassles of endless cost comparisons.

• **AT&T 800 Service.** Like out-of-state WATS service, inter-state 800 service is configured into six service bands starting with those states adjacent to your home state and radiating outward to include the U.S., Puerto Rico, and the U.S. Virgin Islands. You can also sign up for international 800 service that permits toll free calls from Canada and several European and Asian countries.

Costs are based on three rate periods: business day, evening and night/weekend, and are priced according to similar taper points as WATS service. Special features available include: customized call routing (lets you divide your coverage by area codes to establish marketing regions); call allocator (lets you direct a specified percentage of calls to each answering location to improve flow); command routing (reacts to spontaneous needs by redirecting calls to preplanned alternate locations, should overloads occur); time manager and day manager (lets calls be routed to various locations depending on time and day received); call attempt profile (lets you monitor responses by providing you with a printout of all calling attempts to your number); and call prompter (a recorded message informing them of which department might handle their call most effectively). For further details on services and prices, call 800-222-0400.

• **Telephone calling cards.** Rather than fumble for change, the next time you need to place a pay-phone call or make a costly collect call, you might prefer to charge your call on a calling card issued by one of the major carriers. There are over ten thousand pay phones where you can charge calls by placing your AT&T card into a slot. With other phones and cards, you either dial "O," then enter your personal identification number upon hearing a computer tone, or read your ID number to the operator (risky should the wrong person eavesdrop).

Although long distance prices don't vary that substantially

from carrier to carrier, the same is *not* true of these calling card calls. AT&T, for example, adds a $1.05 surcharge to the cost of each call charged on its card; MCI adds 55 cents; and Allnet, ITT, U.S. Sprint and Western Union charge nothing extra. You can get a card and identification number from any carrier offering this service, even if it's not your primary carrier, by calling them up and opening the account. Cards are also available from some local telephone companies as well.

Want your employees to be able to report from the road or out of town whenever necessary without worrying about their incurring card charges for personal calls? Or would you like to offer your special customers the convenience of calling you at your expense without the bother—or higher expense to you—of a collect call? The AT&T "Call Me Card" offers the perfect solution to either of these situations: Though there's an annoying $1.05 surcharge on each call, the user can reach just one number—yours.

HIGH TECH
NETWORKING

- Has the name you've created for a new product already been trademarked by someone else?
- What's the *real* financial lowdown on the company that's just made you an attractive offer for your business?
- Should you take a flyer on the gold mining stock your broker is pushing? How has it performed over the past five years, and what are the experts saying about it now?
- Do the demographics in a neighboring city fit your customer profile, or would you be better off spending your ad dollars in a different market?
- How can you quickly check the background and salary history of an executive you're considering for employment in your firm?

GETTING THE INFORMATION EDGE

The answers to common business questions like these are just minutes away when you team up your personal computer (equipped with a printer and appropriate communications software), a modem and your telephone, and get "online" with one of the more than three thousand electronic databases. Or should you lack a computer, you can arrange for an online search, at modest cost, at many public libraries. (Having your library do a trial search for you could be a good way to explore whether the potential benefits of online searching justify the purchase of a computer for your business.)

It's been estimated that close to 90 percent of the information published over the past ten years is is accessible over telephone lines to computer users. In a single computerized search lasting, say, twenty minutes, you could search through upward of two *million* paragraphs of information, encompassing entries from maybe one thousand magazines and journals and locate the precise facts you need—for less than fifteen dollars.

Here's a short menu of some of the potential profitable data you could be mining with your computer:

• **Business intelligence.** With a few keystrokes, you'd have instant access to the annual reports, quarterly income statements, prospectuses, balance sheets and S.E.C. filings of any publicly held U.S. company, as well as a list of the officers and their salaries. For both public and private companies, you can also scan Dun and Bradstreet reports on 8 million international and U.S. firms (about 60 percent of all companies are included, as well as 80 percent to 90 percent of the more active companies in the U.S.) or obtain a TRW "Business Profiles" credit report containing such data as thirty-, sixty- and ninety-day payment histories, tax liens, judgments, bankruptcies and company background information.

• **In-depth investment guidance.** Do you have an acquisition, merger or stock investment in mind? Ninety seconds after business or financial news breaks, you can be reading it on your screen from the Dow Jones News Service, or you can have instant access to stock, commodity and money market quotes. Other databases offer daily updates on twelve hundred publicly held U.S. firms; five hundred thousand news items on these firms from 1979 forward; the ability to locate all companies with a given price/earnings ratio; business research reports done by top investment bankers and market analysts; and transcripts of such items as interviews with corporate executives and roundtable discussions between industry analysts.

• **Sales opportunities.** The world's biggest customer of goods and services, the U.S. Government, publishes a daily procurement list of supplies and services desired by the forty-five hundred or so federal agencies, titled Commerce Business Daily. By accessing the list online you can have the list scanned in seconds and read exactly what the government wants to buy that your company could sell to it. You can also limit the search to procurement requests from agencies located in your state, if you wish. Another convenient option is to make an initial search, establish the best strategy for identifying sales opportunities within your field of interest, then arrange to have the database vendor send you weekly updates on purchasing plans that fit your business profile.

Want to broaden your selling horizons still further? Two more government-published databases could help: Trade Opportunities lists purchase plans or requests for bids and proposals from governments and companies outside the U.S. and is compiled from information supplied by Foreign Service officers in one hundred thirty countries; and Foreign Traders Index is a compilation of manufacturers, retailers, distributors and others who import from the U.S. or desire to do so. Complete contact information is included.

• **Marketing savvy.** Wondering if someone has already done a marketing study on the demand for a product or service you'd like to introduce? A database directory called FIND/SVP indexes over eleven thousand studies done by five hundred or so American and foreign firms. You can either buy the relevant study from FIND/SVP or learn who's selling it and how much it costs.

A second database aid to your marketing efforts is Donnelly Demographics, which combines U.S. Census material, current year estimates and five-year future projections to help you analyze potential markets by either demographic characteristics or by geographical location.

• **Customized mailing lists.** The Electronic Yellow Pages is a database composed of ten million listings from the yellow-page entries of forty-eight hundred telephone books nationwide, plus such information as 10-K financial reports, census figures, number of employees, assets of banks and savings and loan organizations and other details. This data can be used to compile telemarketing or direct mail prospect lists or to research the size of a market within some particular geographical area.

After selecting your criteria and reviewing sample entries to make sure you're getting appropriate "hits" with your identifiers, you can request the database to print out the entries you've found directly onto your own pressure-sensitive mailing labels or have the database vendor do this for you at their office. A particular advantage of creating a mailing list in this manner is that you can reuse the same list as often as you like without additional fees—unlike those lists provided by list brokers.

• **Government updates.** Concerned that some new regulation or tax code change could affect your business, or do you just need a few fast facts from government information? PRF (short for Government Printing Office Publications Reference File) indexes approximately twenty-five thousand books, pamphlets, maps and other publications distributed free or sold by the U.S. Government, any of which you can order by phone and charge to your credit card by calling the GPO order desk at 202-783-3238.

Federal Register Abstracts database contains such items as: presidential documents, executive orders, summaries of agency rules and regulations, public law notices and information on hearings and meetings. Internal Revenue Service Taxpayer Information covers the current tax year and contains the full text of more than seventy booklets and guides the IRS publishes, along with portions of the book, *Your Federal Income Tax.*

• **Reading for professional or personal growth.** Learn what books, magazine articles and newspaper stories have been written on the topics that interest you. For newspaper and magazine pieces, some databases provide full text you can read online or print out for future reference, while others will mail you a copy of the text of selected articles from their indexes. You may also find that the index summary of the item contains enough background to supply the information you need.

BEHIND THE SCREENS: DATABASE VENDORS

Interested in getting online? Although there are thousands of database vendors, many of them are either electronic bulletin boards established by hobbyists or single-subject databases that may be too specialized for your business needs. Instead, you'll probably appreciate the flexibility and convenience of an account with one of the "supermarket" services that offers you access to a wide variety of different databases under one corporate umbrella.

Here's a list of eight of the major vendors. Before opening an account, you'd be well advised to call each at their toll free

number to get their database catalogs and descriptive brochures, as well as information on current rates.

• **DIALOG Information Service, Inc.**, 3460 Hillview Avenue,
Palo Alto, CA 94304. 800-334-2564 and 415-858-3810. Dialog
has three systems: DIALOG and the DIALOG Business Connection are round-the-clock (except Sundays) services, while
the lower-priced Knowledge Index is accessible only outside of
business hours. DIALOG has over 250 databases, with new
ones being added at the typical rate of thirty to forty a year.

• **BRS Information Technologies,** 1200 Route 7, Latham, NY
12110. 800-227-5277 and 518-738-7251. BRS has three systems: BRS/SEARCH and BRS/BRKTHRU are available from
6:00 A.M. to 4:00 A.M. Monday through Saturday, and Sundays
6:00 A.M. to 2:00 P.M. and 7:00 P.M. to 4:00A.M. The discounted
service, BRS/After Dark operates from 6:00 P.M. to 4:00 A.M.
weekdays and the same hours as the other services on week-
ends. BRS has over one hundred databases online and is
actively adding new ones regularly.

• **Mead Data Central,** 9393 Springboro Pike, P. O. 9933,
Dayton, OH 45401. 800-227-4908. NEXIS, Mead Data's database service, offers full text (rather than bibliographic entries)
of such items as the New York *Times,* "The MacNeil Lerher
News Hour," wire-service reports from sixteen services, over
fifty popular magazines, reports from about thirty brokerage
houses and investment banks and a variety of other sources of
interest to the businessperson. One hundred ten thousand new
documents are added weekly. (The company also offers LEXIS,
a computerized research service oriented to the legal profession.) Weekday hours are 2:15 A.M. to 2:00 A.M. Saturday 2:00
A.M. to 10:00 P.M. and Sunday 6:00 A.M. to 2:00 A.M.

• **ORBIT Search Service,** SDC Information Services, 2500 Colorado Avenue, Santa Monica, CA 90406. 800-421-7229, or 800-352-6689 in California. For European service, contact SDC Information Services, Bakers Court, 4th Floor, Baker Road, Uxbridge, Middlesex UB8 1RG, U.K.; telephone 0895-37137. Offers about sixty-five databases, half of which emphasize technical and scientific material or industry-specific offerings. Monday through Thursday, available except 9:45 P.M. to 10:15 P.M.; Friday 3:00 A.M. to 8:00 P.M. Saturday 8:00 A.M. to 7:00 P.M., and Sunday 7:00 P.M. to 3:00 A.M.

• **Dow Jones News/Retrieval Service,** P.O. Box 300, Princeton, NJ 08540. 800-257-5114, or 609-452-1511 in New Jersey. Keeps you up-to-date with the latest information and quotes on financial markets, lets you do stock trades online via Fidelity Investor's Express, offers shopping services, electronic mail and online banking with New York's Citibank. Also has full text from that day's Wall Street *Journal* online by 6:00 A.M.

• **VU/TEXT Information Services, Inc.,** 1221 Chestnut Street, Philadelphia, PA 19107. 800-258-8080, or 215-665-3300 in Pennsylvania. Also provides access to QL Search, a major Canadian database vendor, via a special password. (QL Search can be contacted at QL Systems, Inc., 112 Kent Street, Suite 1018, Tower B, Ottawa, Ontario K1P 5P2, Canada; 613-238-3499.) Emphasizes databases of local and regional newspapers, also the AP newswire, and sixteen other databases. Available twenty-four hours a day, except for a half-hour during off-peak hours when the system is reloaded.

• **NewsNet, Inc.,** 945 Haverford Road, Bryn Mayr, PA 19010. 800-345-1301, and 215-527-8030 in Pennsylvania. According to Alfred Glossbrenner, author of *How to Look It Up Online* (a most valuable guide to the topic), this service is: "Like single malt Scotch, 'A Prairie Home Companion,' and any book by John McPhee, NewsNet is one of the good things in life . . . it is probably the one online service that virtually all executives, managers and professionals should subscribe to."

The essence of NewsNet is access to over three hundred industry, trade and professional newsletters, covering more than thirty industries. Other databases include four newswire services and TRW credit reports. There's also NewsFlash, a feature which allows customers to specify topics they are interested in and create a customized information package for themselves. You can arrange a free try-out of the system—contact customer service at the number above for particulars. Open twenty-four hours a day.

• **H. W. Wilson Company,** 950 University Avenue, Bronx, NY 10452. 800-622-4002, and 800-538-3888 in New York. Has electronic editions of such well-known Wilson directories as *Reader's Guide to Periodical Literature* (covering 182 popular magazines) and *Biography Index* and fifteen other comprehensive indexes. Open twenty-four hours a day.

U.S. AND INTERNATIONAL ACCESS

Once you've subscribed to a database vendor, you'll typically be supplied with a list of telephone access numbers (consisting of local numbers in all fifty states that gain you access to one of the telecommunications networks, such as Tymnet or Telenet—you pick the number closest to the area in which you are operating), detailed documentation explaining how to enter and use the system, a user number and a secret password. With any good communications software package, you can arrange for your computer to place the call, enter the correct information and log you on to the system. One cautionary note: If you have call waiting service on your telephone, the incoming call signal may cause interference when you're on-line.

For detailed information on the techniques used for efficient online searches, once you've gained entry to the system, you may wish to read either of these excellent guides: *Answers Online*, by Barbara Newlin (McGraw-Hill, 1985) or *How to Look It Up Online*, by Alfred Glossbrenner (St. Martin's Press, 1987).

Should you be planning a trip outside of the U.S. and wish to be able to access your U.S. database vendor, you'll find you can do so with varying degrees of ease from just about anywhere in the global village. In most countries, the telephone and public data services are operated by a government agency known as PTT (Postal, Telegraph and Telephone). By opening an account with them, you'll acquire a "Network User Identifier," or account number, that lets you access the public data handling network in that country. Your call is then routed through that country's national network to an international network and then to a U.S. telecommunications network, such as Tymnet or Telenet, which lets you log on to your database vendor.

To use your U.S. database vendor from abroad, you'll also need a modem conforming to the standards set by the CCITT, Consultative Committee on International Telephone and Telegraph, part of the United Nations. Many U.S.-made modems are compatible with both Bell and CCITT standards. You'll also need the fourteen-digit number that serves as the "address" of both the U.S. telecommunications network and database vendor you wish to reach. Your database vendor should be able to supply you with the correct code, and your communications software can then handle its entry.

For further specifics on the most appropriate method to access your database vendor through the public data telephone services of the particular country where you'll be, you might wish to consult with one of the international specialists at either of these two U.S. telecommunications networks:

International Sales Office
TYMNET/McDonnell Douglas Network Systems
2080 Chainbridge Road
Vienna, VA 22180
800-368-6993
703-356-6993

International Services
Telenet Communications Corporation
12490 Sunrise Valley Drive
Reston, VA 22096
703-689-6300

It's also possible to reach your database vendor from abroad by dialing its direct or incoming WATS number, but this is likely to be more expensive than the procedure outlined above.

ELECTRONIC RENDEZVOUS

To explore the electronic universe accessible by telephone in greater depth, consider subscribing to one of the "telecomputing" services, which offer a wide array of activities and services for both business and consumer use. In addition to gaining access to informational databases, you can exchange E-mail (electronic mail) with thousands of other users, search out shopping services, challenge your brain with an amusing arcade of games or even expand your social horizons by communicating with others who share your professional or personal interests.

Consenting adult computer users can also enjoy a naughtier form of entertainment, sometimes called "CompuSex," during which flirtatious or X-rated messages are exchanged.

(The nickname of "CompuSex" does *not* imply or indicate any connection with the similarly named CompuServe telecomputing service.) Singles can also run electronic "personal" ads on one of the bulletin boards of their telecomputing service and receive electronic billet-doux from would-be suitors. Accessing others' hearts through their keyboards can lead to more permanent connections—at least five couples have married after meeting online.

Here are snapshot profiles of the Big Three in telecomputing and their current services. Access to these services is provided in much the same manner as to the database vendors described earlier, and can also be arranged internationally. For brochures, prices and further information, contact their toll free numbers.

• **The Source**, 1616 Anderson Road, McLean, VA 22102. 800-336-3366, and 703-821-8888 in Virginia. Services are divided into five basic categories. *Databases* now number in excess of eight hundred. *News/weather/sports* includes such offerings as the latest news, available electronically from UPI and AP newswires and the Washington *Post*; general business and financial news and quotes, and a business bulletin board; tax updates; Accu-Weather reports for any city in the U.S., plus local forecasts.

Travel services include the Official Airline Guide, which lists daily arrivals and departures for all of the world's airlines and lets you type in your desired destination and date of departure and scan a list of possible flights, with complete schedule and price information. There's also a travel bulletin board where you can exchange messages and information with others going to or returning from your destination, the Mobil guides to hotels and restaurants and other travel related databases.

Shopping and games includes access to Comp-u-store, an

online catalog service offering an inventory of sixty thousand products such as clothing, sports gear, appliances, electronic equipment and many other products. Or you can unwind with any of dozens of games (none use graphics yet, however).

Communications may be the most stimulating category. You can exchange E-mail with approximately one hundred thousand Source users; join a special-interest group (such as users of IBM and IBM-compatible equipment) to exchange software and news; find others of similar interests on the membership directory to start your own group or do some networking; attend computer conferences on a variety of subjects; and make social or romantic connections through the "chatting feature," where you can paticipate in either a group party line or a discreet private conversation with the partner of your choice.

• **CompuServe Information Service, Inc.**, 5000 Arlington Centre Blvd., Columbus, OH 43220. 800-848-8990, and 614-457-8650 in Ohio. Approximately three hundred and fifty thousand subscribers are now enjoying a huge array of activities and services available on the more than one thousand databases of this network. On the national bulletin board, you'll be able to post or review general-interest messages, such as sale ads, employment opportunities, requests for information and announcements of public meetings. You can also participate in forums and special-interest groups, peek at the pictures on the FBI's "Ten Most Wanted" list or on lists of missing children; plan your vacation and make airline reservations; get a pilot briefing if you'll be doing the flying; and even upgrade your domestic cuisine with cooking tips and recipes.

You'll find an interesting collection of business databases, ranging from flash news and stock quotes, demographic information, DISCLOSURE financials (containing practically every imaginable piece of information an investor could require about a company), and more technical databases. There's also an electronic mall offering a huge range of products; online banking services; opportunities to educate yourself or your children, plus information on colleges and college boards; complete sports/news/weather information; and a variety of games. The CB simulator feature, which is similar to the Source's chatting feature, is like a nightly electronic party and also offers a private conversation mode to exchange intimacies or telephone numbers with compatible conversationalists.

• **Delphi**, General Videotext Corporation, 3 Blackstone Street, Cambridge, MA 02139. 800-544-4005, and 617-491-3393 in Massachusetts. The "main menu" of services includes a number of appetizing offerings.

Business and financial services include AP business news and Japan Economic Newswire; the Business Wire, with press releases from companies around the world announcing new products, personnel changes and other corporate changes; stock and commodity quotes; Dow Jones averages; an electronic newsletter, *Investor*; Security Objective Service (stock advisory reports by investment experts); and business forums for a variety of industries, where members can trade news and business software with one another. You can also place classified help-wanted or situation-wanted ads.

Delphi mail offers TII translation service, where your message can be translated into any of six languages—handy since Delphi subscribers now include residents of forty different countries. A "mail-thru" feature lets you communicate with CompuServe users and telex users as well as other Delphi subscribers.

The *library* offers the services of an online librarian who'll research just about any topic or answer quick questions online; access to DIALOG and the Kussmaul Encyclopedia; Computerized AIDS Information Network (with latest news and research findings); and full-text entries from several computer and telecommunications magazines.

Conferencing offers both open and private conversations with other members; forums; special-interest groups (some of the more popular are groups for users of just about every personal computer brand, electronic musicians, writers, sci-fi fans and computer artists). During the special-interest conferences it's possible to download software you wish to share with other members and to have your technical questions answered by experts.

Along with similar travel and shopping services as CompuServe and the Source, you'll also find such innovations as an online gourmet, wine reports and many entertainment options, including adventure, board, logic and trivia games; astrological forecasts and biorhythms; and the chance to show off your creative talents by writing a portion of a member-written collaborative novel.

INFORMATION BROKERS

Wondering if there's an easier way to enjoy access to the high tech universe? Should you lack the time or inclination to do your own online searches or require assistance in mastering the most cost-effective and efficient procedures, an option to consider is engaging the services of an information broker. While there are said to be more than one thousand individuals or companies offering such services, one *caveat* is that qualifications and experience levels can vary widely in this field—making it essential to investigate the background of anyone you're considering hiring.

There are several ways to locate the right information broker for your needs. In addition to using the online search service of your library (if available), you can sometimes arrange to hire a research librarian to work for you on a freelance basis. If you subscribe to one of the telecomputing services, you might also try putting a notice listing your data requirements on the appropriate special-interest bulletin board.

There are also at least two specialized directories you might wish to consult. The first, *Marquis Who's Who Directory of Online Professionals*, is published in print and electronic editions. You can either buy the book through your bookstore or its publishers, read it at the library or scan it online through DIALOG (a far cheaper alternative). The book includes information brokers and others who provide a variety of online services.

The *Directory of Fee-Based Information Services*, published by Burwell Enterprises, 5106 F.M. 1960 West, Suite 349, Houston, TX 77069; telephone 713-537-9051, is an annually updated volume, organized geographically by state or country, listing information brokers. The directory contains about seven hundred entries (though the number is expected to grow rapidly in future years) from over thirty countries. Each entry includes the company's name, personnel, areas of specialization and a description of services available. The book's indexes list brokers by city, company name, personnel names, service and subject area.

Burwell Enterprises also publishes a bimonthly newsletter, *Information Broker*. Anyone who either buys the directory or subscribes to the newsletter can contact the organization to get a free referral to an information broker who'll meet their needs. Nonsubscribers can also use this matchmaking service by paying a modest fee.

Here are capsule descriptions of three large information brokers. For further information on services, prices and areas of expertise, contact the organizations at the telephone number or address specified in the entry.

• **Information on Demand, Inc.**, P.O. Box 9550, Berkeley, CA 94709. 800-227-0750, and 415-644-4500 in California. This full-service research organization has a search department and a document delivery department. Staffers are full-time professional researchers, many of whom have MLS (Master of Library Science) degrees. Basically, the firm provides customized research from secondary sources (published materials, in other words), using online searches (they maintain accounts at more than a dozen vendors) and traditional manual research methods, like phone interviews or library visits. Your research can be delivered either as a written report, on a floppy disk or even downloaded directly onto your computer system. You can hire the company by contacting the number above or through The Source.

• **FIND/SVP**, 625 Avenue of the Americas, New York, NY 10011. 212-645-4500. Not only has this company created the database of market study reports mentioned earlier in this chapter, but it's also one of the biggest information brokers and claims to have established the world's largest private business library. The document retrieval division can not only provide copies of any books, articles or reports desired, but can also provide such offbeat items as product samples, theater tickets, and in one case, the front end of a 1977 Toyota.

The search division, which subscribes to several hundred databases, offers both Quick Information Service for questions requiring only a few hours of research, and Strategic Research when a more extensive investigation is required. The actual searching is handled by specialists in such areas as: consumer, health care, industrial/technical, business/financial; and a central research group which tackles biographic, demographic, political, publishing and arts-related topics and other topics not covered by other groups. There's also a translation service and an Information Tracking Service which keeps you up-to-date on any specified subject. The firm charges its clients a monthly retainer based on the amount of usage, plus its out-of-pocket expenses.

• **R.I.C.E (Regional Information Communications Exchange)**, Fondren Library, Rice University, P.O. Box 1892, Houston, TX 77251. 713-528-3553. A number of larger universities have entered the information brokering business—some others are Georgia Tech and University of Washington—and these academic organizations can sometimes represent a better bargain to the consumer than the commercially operated firms. Fees tend to be lower since academic information brokers often calculate their fees to cover overhead and expenses rather than to generate profits. And you get the services of highly trained academic researchers, with access both to online databases and the full resources of the affiliated university's own library or, in some cases, their special collections of doctoral theses, letters or unpublished manuscripts, rare books, or other unique items.

15

FUTURE PHONING

Imagine yourself lifting the receiver to call an associate in a distant city and having the power to simultaneously view each other on a video screen, exchange important documents or computer data and talk—all on the same telephone line. As you converse, your phone might be screening other calls— diplomatically refusing calls from long-winded or unpleasant contacts, giving top priority to that call-back from the venture capitalist who's financing your latest project. Or you might program it to audibly announce the name and number of each caller before you answer, letting you decide whether to take the call personally or let it ring through to an assistant.

Should important business—or a much deserved vacation—send you out of town or out of the country, suppose you could program any nearby phone just by punching in your home or office number, to ring you when calls to either of those locations come in for you. Or imagine yourself skiing in the Alps, knowing that your wristwatch will instantly alert you if any vital telephone calls or messages come for you.

While these futuristic scenarios may sound like mere phone fantasies, actually they're based on technology or services that are currently in the testing stages. Within the next ten years—or less—your telephone may be part of a global "smart" network that will multiply its communications capabilities dramatically. Here's a tour through the rewired world of tomorrow—as it is taking shape from today's designers and engineers.

THE "WONDER PHONE"

A current hot button in the telephone business is creating a mass market version of the home information services popularized by telecomputing vendors like CompuServe. Pacific Bell has been offering some of its subscribers the chance to participate in a free trial of its system, Project Victoria, which lets users tap into such services as MCI Communications Corp.'s electronic mail, Dow Jones and Co.'s newswires, home banking with Bank of America and a community bulletin board announcing school activities and town council meetings, plus thirty informational databases—all on a free trial basis, using loaned Macintosh computers supplied by Apple Computers, Inc.

Among the applications consumers of the service had devised during the test were: sending electronic cards, congratulatory messages and other personal correspondence for instant delivery and writing a romance novel titled *The Great American Novel,* online. The potential business applications include: verification of credit card accounts; real estate multiple-listing databases; creating a local area network of the personal computers within a company; over-the-phone readings of electrical and gas meters; monitoring the medical condition of patients and improved security against fire and burglars for homes and offices.

The powerful potential of the system comes from a "black box" that splits a single, conventional phone line into seven channels, two for voice and five for data. Four of the data channels are equipped for relatively slow speed digital transmissions, while the fifth sends digital data eight times faster, making it more useful for transmitting computer pictures in color, for example. Members of a family or office with the black box could hold two entirely different telephone conversations on the voice channels, while the five data channels were zipping information from your computer to your branch offices or customers.

While the prices for this service, should it become widely available, have yet to be announced, Bell officials say that the extra channels will cost less than extra phone lines, while the participating database vendors will charge separately for access to their systems.

THE DIGITAL CONNECTION

Unquestionably the most ambitious telephone project in the works is the current effort to design and implement a worldwide, homogeneous network that will run on an entirely new transmission technology—known as integrated digital networks. In terms of its potential impact on the telephone industry, such an advance might be considered equivalent to converting from a horsedrawn buggy to a Ferrari or from hot lead printing to computerized typesetting.

At present, the telephone system is an amalgam of advanced technology, such as state-of-the art digital switches (that route your call to the correct destination), microwave radio equipment, satellites and high-capacity optical glass cable; and low tech older equipment, such as low capacity copper wires and costly conversion gear that lets the old and new technologies function together. It's expensive to run and relatively inefficient to use—particularly for data transmission, which now accounts for ten-percent of telephone use.

The telephone system was orginally designed to carry voice communications, which it handles through *analog* transmission, a system of carrying signals as electric waves that move along the wires. (It's called analog because these waves are analogous to sound waves.) Data, which starts out as digital signals, must also be converted into analog form (that's what a modem does) in order to be carried through the system. One flaw in this system we've all encountered is that any electrical interference along the line will change the shape of the waves— which you hear as annoying static.

Digital transmissions, on the other hand, consist of a dense stream of pulses representing either "on" or "off" states inside a computer's silicon chips (these are equivalent to binary ones and zeros). Not only does digital transmission preserve clarity, but it eliminates several cumbersome—and costly— steps in sending data. Right now, to transport information online, you'd first use a modem to convert it to analog form. Part-way along the journey, the data would arrive at one of the telephone company's switches and be converted back to digital form. Next, it would be turned back to analog signals to complete the trip, and finally it would be converted once again to digital by the modem on the other end of the line. It's small wonder that experts say you'd be able to send and receive data seven-hundred-percent faster on an all-digital system!

Before a global all-digital network can be implemented, a set of uniform standards for the hardware and software to be installed in the system must be agreed upon. A design skeleton for a system named Integrated Services Digital Network (ISDN) was arrived at in 1984 by a division of the International Telecommunications Union, an organization of the world's phone companies. Several telephone companies—among them eight of the U.S.'s Baby Bells, the national phone companies of Britain and Japan, West Germany's Bundepost and Canada's Telecom—are conducting technical and marketing trials of digital systems, though not all of them are using the ISDN design.

In the U.S., the first trial of an ISDN system is taking place at McDonald's Corporation headquarters in Illinois. The fast-food company is using it to send thousands of messages between phones, data terminals, personal computers and fascimile machines without any costly rewiring of its offices. Other phone companies will be scheduling trials at giant corporations like Shell Oil in the near future; and a few adventurous companies have purchased their own, private ISDN systems.

Competition among companies scrambling for the $450-million-a-year U.S. Government long distance services contract has increased the momentum toward ISDN. The Government has specified that all equipment used for the job of linking up 1.3 million telephones within three thousand five hundred different federal offices must be ISDN-compatible. Whichever supplier wins the bidding for history's largest telephone project will also be developing advanced features such as state-of-the-art electronic mail and video teleconferencing capacities, which may well set the standards for the telephones all of us will be using in the future.

Should ISDN pan out in these tests, cities such as New York, Chicago and Los Angeles may be converted to the system by 1990, saving local businesses billions in wiring and computer costs, while giving both business and residential customers access to state-of-the-art services.

Here's what ISDN might offer to you and your business:

• **High speed data transport.** This is almost certain to be *the* most urgent consumer and business telecommunications need in the near future. Already, sales of online electronic information have reached an annual volume of $1.6 *billion* in the U.S. alone. A few years from now, says Judge Harold H. Green, who presided over the AT&T divestiture trial, "Information will be to this period what steel and coal were fifty years ago." Industry analysts project that businesses, which currently spend just 0.4 percent of their revenues on information, will find themselves investing 500 percent more money in maintaining their information edge. Predicts an expert: "Everyone will have his finger on the trigger, so you will have to be that much quicker on the draw."

Ultimately, a crucial objective of the new system, according to MCI Communications Corporation's chairman, William G. McGowan, is to make this future a reality. "We're combining computing power, information and telecommunications into a transportation system for the information age."

• **Single-line efficiency.** Another key advantage to the business consumer is that voices, video images and computer data could be transmitted along the same telephone line simultaneously, rather than a separate line being required for each function, as in the present system. During the course of a single call, you could provide the other person with a fax of your proposed contract, spreadsheets of costs and video images of the design, while smoothly explaining how all of these intersect into an exciting business opportunity for the two of you. Moreover, no modems would be required to get online, and previously incompatible computer systems could now "talk" to one another.

• **Sophisticated services.** Your telephone will be increasingly programmable. You might opt to refuse calls from certain parties, getting off the hook with a tactful recording; arrange to have an ongoing conversation interrupted should an urgent call you're expecting come in; have the name and number of callers announced electronically before you answer; receive written messages from callers who reach your telephone during your absence; and be able to enjoy easier and more extensive access to electronic banking and shopping, videotex information and voice and electronic mail.

Another intriguing possibility: An individual calling number that's assigned to you rather than to your home or office phone. Your personal account number could travel with you wherever you go, allowing you to program any nearby phone to let you receive your calls or bill outgoing calls to your account at local rates. Not only would your number follow you on your travels, but you might even be able to inform phone company computers of your day-to-day schedule weeks in advance, should you so desire.

• **Lower costs.** While the exact costs of ISDN service have yet to be announced—phone companies have provided them free in their technical and marketing trials—it's anticipated that businesses will realize a huge savings on telecommunications costs. Rather than pay several networks, as some companies do, to handle their voice traffic, data communications, local area computer networks, and fascimile transmissions, they would have less expensive and more efficient service with one all-digital network. The Boeing Company, with its seventy thousand phones, expects the ISDN-like equipment it's installing to slash its telephone costs by $150 million over the next ten years.

Smaller consumers will also benefit—even if they don't have extensive telecommunications needs. That's because our telephone companies can automate their services and reduce operating costs. Just by replacing live operators with electronic voices to handle collect calls, for example, regional Bell companies would save $250 million a year. Business customers would also find their express mail and messenger costs drastically reduced—or perhaps eliminated entirely.

• **The electronic phone company.** How would you like a phone that fixes itself before you even notice a service problem? With ISDN in place, the phone company's computers could monitor service more carefully and automatically initiate repairs over phone lines—dropping repair costs and improving reliability. Many of your other telephone service needs could also be handled by computer, rather than expensive live personnel. By dialing a special 800 number, you might, in the future, be able to place your equipment orders or requests for other telephone company services with its computer, just by pressing the right buttons on your handset.

Another potential gain is more efficient routing of calls. With ISDN you might no longer suffer the annoyance of hearing a recorded voice intone, "All long distance lines are busy at the moment. Please try your call later." Computers at the phone companies would be quicker to identify potential traffic jams—and to reroute your calls.

• **Entrepreneurial opportunities.** You could profit from the all-digital network in a variety of ways. Currently the Baby Bells are developing a system called the Intelligent Network, which would use small, self-contained computer systems and a special signalling system to tie into the ISDN network. Software dealers could use this system to market and deliver their product entirely by phone—eliminating the expense of maintaining retail outlets.

Another potential hot spot is the business of tying office computers together into local area networks, though some phone companies are making their own aggressive entry into this field. Nynex, the holding company for New York Telephone Company, is reaching out to the business customer with its Intellihub digital service that runs private high speed data lines between offices.

Southern Bell is starting work with housing developers to

offer cable TV service to new subdivisions that is transmitted by phone lines rather than coaxial cables.

• **Video phones.** Not only could your telephone be bringing in your TV service, but it could provide video images of you and the person on the other end of the line. The signals that make up TV or video images can also be transmitted as binary bits—and the higher speed of an all-digital system could make it feasible to conduct "show and tell" presentations of your product by phone, keep a sharp eye on your negotiating opponent or just add the visual dimension to your business or social calls.

• **Electronic mail and publishing.** Although limited electonic mail services now exist—customers of CompuServe or MCI Mail can exchange text files with a pool of five-hundred-thousand users—much of the potential of this medium of communication has yet to be exploited. The chairman of Lotus Development Corporation, Jim Manzi, has been quoted as saying that new developments will help make "instant electronic communications an everyday event."

While there are currently 5 million electronic mailboxes in the U.S.—3.7 million of them belonging to internal systems set up by corporations for their employees—in the future we may find ourselves able to send a document, picture or spreadsheet easily and cheaply to virtually any business associate, anywhere in the world. With ubiquitous electronic mailboxes, you'd never again endure the annoyances of lost or delayed mail or endless rounds of telephone tag with hard-to-reach associates.

You could also target your advertising and promotional efforts more effectively, delivering up-to-the-minute information to you customers and prospects at low cost. And, by combining electronic mail with the low-cost existing "desktop" publishing technology, those of a literary bent could distribute and sell newsletters, magazines, newspapers or even full-length books electronically.

• **Party Lines.** One current development that seems destined to become even more popular in the future is the reintroduction of the old-fashioned party line—with a twist. Now known somewhat grandiosely as voice teleconferencing or voice-bridging services, these "chat lines," which might be considered the telephone counterpart of citizen's band radio, allow up to ten callers to socialize with one another. Company moderators act as chaperones, keeping the talk reasonably clean and filling any gaps in the conversation.

Recently British Telecom introduced a U.S. version of its Talkabout service, which has enjoyed four years of success in Britain. The company anticipates that its U.S. service, now available in Boston, will generate upward of a million calls in the first two months, each averaging a six-minute, seventy-cent chat. The local phone company pockets 60 percent of the revenue and British Telecom gets the rest. Party lines are also catching on in California and New York and may soon be offered in several other states.

Another variation on this theme is a device called Videotel, which will soon be offered in the U.S. by CTL Communications. In France, four million of these screen-and-keyboard devices, which send messages over phone lines, have been distributed free by the government—allowing citizens to access computerized shopping and stock information, along with other services. Here, for the price of a local call, those who purchase the machine will be able to make social connections with such services as "Bar," where one can see such generic pick-up lines as "Male or female?" on one's screen.

After trying Minitel, an experimental version of the machine, *New York* magazine journalist David Blum wrote:

"There's nothing like coming home after a hard day's work, turning on the Minitel, and discovering that someone named Natasha wants to know what I'm wearing."

Whether or not Videotel becomes the latest phone fad, there's one safe prediciton to be made: The entrepreneurs of the future are sure to become increasingly inventive in their search for new ways to ring up extra dollars from dialing.

16

CHARISMATIC CALLING

Want to add extra sizzle to *your* future phoning? The real secret of a powerful phone personality is a charismatic style that compels attention while keeping potential challengers at bay. Infusing your conversation with this magical fire ignites others' imaginations, making your ideas, projects, deals and dreams acquire larger-than-life-sized proportions in the audience's minds. They are drawn by the aura of power and success that radiates through your words and thoughts.

Acquiring charisma takes courage. Thomas P. Watson, past president and chairman of IBM, once suggested an unusual formula for success: "Double your rate of failure." What fascinates us about charismatic individuals is their willingness to dream big dreams and take big risks to make them work. This daring spirit is what hooks the audience; the suspense of seeing the wire-walker undertake his perilous crossing. Our darker side envisions, not entirely unpleasantly, the blood on the floor; another part of us longs to share the triumph of emerging unscathed.

Another crucial ingredient is a drop-dead confidence. With that, even a small dream and a small risk can be very arousing to others. Inspire yourself with a sincere enthusiasm for what you are doing, and others will want to warm themselves in the glow of your belief. Further convince yourself that the best is yet to come, and others will be attracted by the force of the magnetic vision that irresistibly draws you onward and upward.

Here are some ways to increase your calling charisma:

• **Sound like a leader.** The Delphic Oracle of mythology, which may be the ultimate voice of authority, rumbled the earth as its terrible voice issued from the depths of the shrine. We still hear the ring of command in a slow, deep voice, especially one that speaks infrequently but with force. A leader lets others explain their problems and reveal their needs, then uses a few decisive words to impart his predictions, plans and opinions.

• **Project passion.** For a cool medium, use a hot message, says media expert Marshall McLuhan. Advertisers have long exploited the power of emotional or sexy language to penetrate our defenses and resonate in our minds. Stockbrokers titillate a lust to buy with such descriptions as: "This stock is a potential doubler; a hot little quickie you can get in and out of in a hurry." In his book, *Secrets of a Corporate Headhunter*, John Wareham describes how he used sexy talk to plant powerful *negative* ideas about his rivals' business practices: "Sometimes, [the big New York search firms] find themselves *in bed with your competition*."

Stirring, charismatic speech requires subtle choices; consider the different emotions stimulated by the two words "problem" and "challenge." The hottest words usually touch upon a fundamental human drive: escaping danger and violence, satisfying hunger and thirst, obtaining sexual fulfillment, nurturing a home and family and ensuring one's continued survival. Add one of these potent concepts to your idea and you'll have a formula for instant, hot communication.

• **Sell fantasies**. "Basically we're selling dreams, hope in a bottle," a Revlon executive once told me. Another entrepreneur, who sells lingerie through home parties, maintains that the basis of her fortune is "X-rated fantasies." Most people, says this businesswoman, have no fantasies, X-rated or otherwise, and will pay extravagantly for a bit of ready-made romance.

Even when the product is yourself, a touch of fantasy adds sizzle. A young architect I know enjoys a reputation for genius, despite her consistently average work, because of her intriguing image as a woman with a tragic past. While no one has actually penetrated her secret, if there is one, her self-portrait of a suffering artist has proved so attractive to clients that she's become rich.

• **Be mysterious and unpredictable**. Although I have received literally thousands of phone calls from prospective clients, only one struck me as truly magical. During the summer doldrums a few years ago, a mysterious stranger called me and said that a psychic had predicted that an agent with the letters "C" and "L" in her name would sell every book he wrote, with absolutely no effort, because work would always come looking for him. This offbeat approach amused me, and I asked to see his book. The day it arrived—before I'd even opened the package—a paperback editor called and offered to buy the book, *sight unseen*. Magic or an elaborate humbug? Fondling my commission check, I wondered all the way to the bank . . .

The telephone is the ideal magician's prop. At one large

travel company executives instruct their secretaries merely to tell callers that they are "away," leaving others to wonder if they're setting up a tour of the North Pole or only visiting the coffee machine. An unlisted number, given out with appropriate rituals, hints that you are unavailable and much sought after.

Additional drama can be added by calling at unexpected hours, catching the other person unprotected by his secretary as he eats at his desk or sneaks in early; or in an unexpected ways, by making some calls with magnificent pomp and secretarial ceremony, others from a pay phone or from an esoteric part of the world. Sprinkle the conversation with an occasional cryptic comment, a suggestion of secret sources of information, a bit of mysterious silence or a poignant sigh now and then, and the listener will invent the rest.

• **Be disarmingly frank.** Paradoxically, revelatory remarks add to your mystery. Your audience feels your sincerity, but is never sure if you are really telling all. Instead, the scraps of truth you offer feed their fantasies by offering appetizing new lines of speculation. Telling others the truth about themselves is also powerful; people are always fascinated by the prospect of seeing themselves through another's eyes, especially in a flattering but basically realistic light.

• **Act ruthlessly when necessary.** The wise prince, Machiavelli wrote, would rather be feared than loved. The charismatic leader also recognizes the importance of a show of force, but reserves it as a tactic of last resort. He avoids the gratuitous intimidation that inspires resentment but is respected because his threats are *not* idle. He's dangerous because his actions aren't decided upon in the heat of emotion but under the cool control of reason.

• **Exit gracefully**. The climactic moment in a magician's act is his sudden disappearance. The audience stares at the empty stage and wonders where reality ends and make-believe takes over. Some charismatic callers have the same trick: Rather than linger over the formalities, they wind up their business with a snappy line or two, and vanish. No good-byes; just a concluding click, and they have disappeared.

BIBLIOGRAPHY

Bly, Amy Sprecher and Robert, W. *Information Hotline U.S.A.* NAL Penguin, Inc. 1987.

Boyan, Lee. *Successful Cold Call Selling.* ANACOM. 1983.

Brownstone, David M. *Sell Your Way to Success.* John Wiley & Sons, Inc. 1979.

Bowling, Evelyn Burge. *Voice Power.* Stackpole Books. 1980.

Bury, Charles. *Telephone Techniques that Sell.* Warner Books, Inc. 1980.

City Cross-Reference Directory. Cole Publications. Annual.

Cohen, Herb. *You Can Negotiate Anything.* Citadel Press. 1980.

Consumer Resource Handbook. Available free by writing to Consumer Information Center, Pueblo, CO 81009.

Directory of Fee-Based Information Services. Burwell Enterprises. Annual.

Gale's Encyclopedia of Associations. Gale Research Company. New editions periodically.

Glossbrenner, Alfred. *How to Look It Up Online.* St. Martin's Press. 1987.

Marquis Who's Who Directory of Online Professionals. Marquis Who's Who. 1984.

Ling, Mona. *How to Increase Sales and Put Yourself Across by Telephone.* Prentice-Hall, Inc. 1963.

Masser, Barry Z. and Leeds, William M. *Power-Selling by Telephone.* Parker Publishing Company, Inc. 1983.

McCormack, Mark H. *What They Don't Teach You at Harvard Business School:* Notes From a Street Smart Executive. Bantam Books. 1985.

Dun and Bradstreet's Million Dollar Directory. Dun and Bradstreet, Inc. Annual.

Newlin, Barbara. *Answers Online.* McGraw-Hill, Inc. 1985.

Potter, Stephen. *Complete Upsmanship.* The New American Library, Inc. 1970.

Ries, Al and Trout, Jack. *Positioning: The Battle for Your Mind*. Warner Books. 1981.

Schiffman, Stephen. *Cold Calling Techniques (That Really Work)*. Bob Adams, Inc. 1987.

Shafiroff, Martin D. and Shook, Robert L. *Successful Telephone Selling in the '80s*. Barnes and Noble Books. 1982.

Standard and Poor's Register of Corporations, Directors and Executives. Standard and Poor's Corporation. Annual.

Stone, Bob and Wyman, John. *Successful Telemarketing*. NTC Business Books. 1986.

Thomas Register of American Manufacturers, Thomas Publishing Company. Annual.

Trahey, Jane. *Jane Trahey on Women and Power*. Rawson Associates Publishers, Inc. 1977.

Wareham, John. *Secrets of a Corporate Headhunter*. PEI Books, Inc. 1980.

Ziglar, Zig. *Zig Ziglar's Secrets of Closing the Sale*. Berkley Books, 1984.